What Others Are Saying...

"John Fischer is right on when he says that as Christians we cannot huddle for safety in our subculture. We are commanded to go into the world to proclaim and live out the gospel. *Fearless Faith* is an excellent guide to doing just that. Taking a stand for the gospel will always put us at odds with an unbelieving world, and God does not require us to avoid controversy even if it were possible. Read this book and learn what it means to live fearlessly in faith."

Charles W. Colson
Chairman
Prison Fellowship Ministries
Washington, DC

"I love John and I love his writing. *Fearless Faith* is the right book for our times."

Steve Arterburn
Founder of New Life Ministries and Women of Faith

"Fischer fearlessly takes on sacred cows...even the ones who provide his milk, in this provocative call to followers of Christ to live the gospel out rather than 'selling' it. The notion that Christians can sometimes obscure the true meaning of Christianity or that seemingly uncompromising language can actually compromise the message of the gospel are conundrums worth exploring. *Fearless Faith* is an uncomfortably articulate wake-up-call to the Christian subculture."

John W. Styll
Founder of *CCM* magazine

"A timely and winsome word of challenge for 'such a time as this!' John Fischer calls us to abandon the safe worlds we have tried to create and urges us to 'step out of the boat and engage the culture around us with faith free from all the trappings of a 'religious' subculture. Everyone interested in being salt and light in the world should read this engaging work!"

Steve G. W. Moore, Ph.D.
Senior Vice President
Asbury Theological Seminary

"John Fischer cracks open the comfortable cocoon that pop-Christianity has woven for itself and exposes us to the dangerous but exhilarating light of true Christ-likeness."

Rod Robison
Vice President of Constituent Services
Family Life Radio Network

"For a number of years—both in person and in print—I have been impressed by John Fischer's clarion call for Christians to inhabit the marketplace of ideas instead of a Christian subculture; to serve their neighbors instead of treating them as evangelism projects; to walk in humility instead of pursuing political power. Though others have joined in sounding the alarms regarding the dangers of Christian subculture, few do it with John's nuance and conviction. More than ever, the American Christian church needs books such as *Fearless Faith*."

Dr. Tom Jennings
Director of Worship Arts
Redeemer Presbyterian Church
New York City

"Years ago Daniel Barhaus wrote: 'Make no little plans...they have no magic to stir men's blood.' John Fischer has written clearly and well in *Fearless Faith*. His words and ideas will stir you to make no little plans about how you can have a greater impact on your neighborhood and your world."

Peter Herschend
Vice Chairman and Co-owner
Silver Dollar City, Inc.
Branson, MO

"Brilliant and thought-provoking...John's writing challenges us to be intelligent Christians. He is not afraid to ask the 'tough' questions...and God has given him answers that will help all of us grow as Christians."

Tom Brooks
New Earth Productions, Inc.

FEARLESS FAITH

JOHN FISCHER

HARVEST HOUSE PUBLISHERS
Eugene, Oregon 97402

Cover by Left Coast Design, Portland, Oregon

Project Editor: Terry Glaspey

FEARLESS FAITH
Copyright © 2002 by John Fischer
Published by Harvest House Publishers
Eugene, Oregon 97402

Library of Congress Cataloging-in-Publication Data
Fischer, John, 1947–.
    Fearless faith / John Fischer
        p. cm.
    Includes bibliographical references.
    ISBN 0-7369-0747-5
    1. Faith. 2. Christian life. I. Title.

    BV4637 .F48 2002
    269'.2—dc21   2001039719

Printed in the United States of America

03 04 05 06 / BP-MS / 10 9 8 7 6 5 4 3 2

CONTENTS

I am the gate; whoever enters through me will be saved. He will come in and go out, and find pasture.

—JESUS (JOHN 10:9)

Introduction

———— ✺ ————

September 11, 2001, was a turning point for America. On that peaceful late-summer day, simultaneous acts of terrorism wreaked wartime destruction on human life and property. Something changed that day, and all Americans noticed it. We lost our belief in our invulnerability, our sense of safety, our casual air of going about our business. Whatever all this meant and would later mean, one thing was for sure, nothing would ever be the same.

The following week I turned in the manuscript of this book and found that these events had underlined the immediacy of the book's message. This book is all about safety and danger. It is about the sense of safety that Christians have felt while tucked away in a subculture of our own making. It is about how pursuing that safety runs counter to the purposes of Christ in sending us into the world, where we *should* be in danger.

The ease with which these acts of terrorism were carried out and the ensuing difficulty in finding and bringing to justice those who were responsible ensure that it will be some time before we breathe any collective sigh of relief in relation to enemies such as these, if we ever do. We discovered our sense of safety was no more than a myth, an illusion. But losing our illusions may not have been such a bad thing. It awakened us to reality, and even if that reality is painful, we are better off embracing it than lying to ourselves.

In the same way, we need to wake up to the reality of the world we live in as Christians and realize that the safe Christian subculture we've been working so hard to build is an illusion as well. It's essential, in fact, for us to awaken to this truth. To think we are safe when we are not is to perpetuate a false security. I would suggest that we as Christians need to learn to *embrace* the danger of living in a dangerous world and trust not a safe subculture to protect us, but a praying Savior. Only then can we go into the world as Christ has sent us: with hope and a fearless faith, and a mission to love, serve, and manifest the good news of Jesus Christ.

CHAPTER ONE

The Prayer of Jesus

---⌇---

A Dying Man's Request

You could say it was a dying man's last request—the last will and testament of the Son of God. To whom is he going to leave his inheritance? Who is going to carry out God's will on earth, and with what will they do it? There is no gold tucked away in a Jerusalem vault, no Swiss bank account to hand over. His resources are not of this world. That is why his prayer is so important.

Jesus has invested his life for the world and is about to pour out his last drop of blood for its salvation. But what Jesus will do after that is just as remarkable. He is about to delegate the kingdom of God. He's going to hand over his personal possession—his labor of love and sacrifice—to someone else. Someone else will continue the work he began. Like a starting pitcher who has held the opposing team scoreless through eight innings of a one-run ball game, Jesus is standing on the mound, waiting to hand the ball to some rookie reliever sauntering in from the bull pen, chewing on a wad of gum.

No wonder he prayed so hard that night.

"I will remain in the world no longer, but they are still in the world, and I am coming to you" (John 17:11).

That would be us. He's talking about you and me—all believers in him. We are the ones with the ball now. And he gave it to us with the bases loaded and nobody out. It's a dangerous situation to inherit.

"I have given them your word and the world has hated them" (John 17:14).

The world was not a friendly place for Jesus and his followers. Following Jesus meant putting oneself at risk. Protection was paramount in his prayer, both while he was here and after he was gone.

"Holy Father, protect them by the power of your name—the name you gave me—so that they may be one as we are one. While I was with them, I protected them and kept them safe" (John 17:11-12).

It must have been comforting to have known his presence. To know you were safe because Jesus was there with you. He was there in the boat when the storm came, there in the crowd when the riot broke out, there when your best friend died, there when the Pharisees grew angry, there when the demons came out. The disciples had little to fear when he was around. But he wouldn't always be there. He was going away. What would they do without him? More important: What do *we* do without his physical presence, for we are the ones he is really thinking about here when he prays.

"My prayer is not for them alone. I pray also for those who will believe in me through their message" (John 17:20).

That would be us, of course.

"My prayer is not that you take them out of the world but that you protect them from the evil one (John 17:15).

Ah yes, there it is—the part of his prayer that tells us what to expect. This is where he reveals what he intends to do, and not do, for us. And what he *won't* do is as important as what he will. He doesn't intend for us to be removed from the world, but to be protected in the middle of it. He doesn't want us removed from danger, he wants us surrounded by danger on every hand—but safe from the evil one.

It is important to realize, in our current dilemma, that the prayers of Jesus are more effective than ours. Our prayers are attached to our human need, a limited view of our situation, and the options we have for relief. Sometimes our prayers are no more than wishes. The prayers of Jesus, on the contrary, are completely in accord with God's will because he and the Father are one. If Jesus prays for our protection, then it is because he knows God fully intends to protect us. And if he prays for us not to be removed from the world, it is because he has no intention of rescuing us out of the world. This is not a well-intentioned wish on the part of Jesus. It is the will of God to leave us in the world and meet us with all the provisions and protection we need to be here and be involved in the world. Anything short of this is less than what God intends for us.

Two things are clear about these petitions from the last request of a dying man who also happens to be the Son of God. The first is that he expects us to be in the world, and the second is that in doing so we will be in danger. Apparently Jesus has no intention of relieving us of the cause of that danger. There would be no need for him to pray for our protection if this were not so. Notice also that there are no qualifiers to this statement—as in "keep the world from getting too bad so it isn't so hard on them." No matter how bad the world gets, he still wants us in it.

I suppose people could get a little upset at Jesus for this if they wanted to. It's a little like falling into a well and having someone yell down from the top, "Don't worry down there. I'm praying for you." *Gee thanks,* we would want to say. *Why don't you try pulling me up?* Of course we would not really say this because it's Jesus up there, and it would sound as if we were accusing him of not knowing what he was doing. It can be somewhat disconcerting, though, when you think that Jesus could easily rescue us from our worldly predicament but doesn't.

A Separate World

This last will and testament of Jesus seems to defy a long-standing tradition: the separation of Christians from the world and worldly things in order to remain pious and pure. This doctrine of separation has its roots in tradition rather than in Scripture. The biblical doctrine of separation has primarily to do with what happens in one's mind and heart. For instance, later in this prayer, Jesus prays for us to be sanctified (set apart) by the truth of God's word. Since knowing God's word is an inner reality, this injunction would apply to a spiritual separation, not a physical pulling away from culture and society, a mind-set, not a physical movement. Likewise, when Paul tells us in Romans 12:2 not to be conformed to the pattern of this world but to be transformed "by the renewing of your mind," it is an appeal to a different way of thinking, not to a change of address.

I grew up entrenched in this doctrine of separation, so I understand how threatening it can be to let go of it. I can still remember when as a small child I fingered a little sculpture my parents used to keep on a shelf over the kitchen sink. It was of three monkeys. One had his hands over his eyes; one had his hands over his ears; and one had his hands over his mouth. "See no evil; hear no evil; speak no evil" was the message it conveyed. This thinking was very popular among Christians at the time, and it helped justify our separation from the world. That separation took on the form of cultural abstinence (no movies, clubs, or theaters) and behavioral taboos (no dancing, card playing, or makeup).

We were to keep ourselves separate from the world in order to be fully committed Christians. Scriptural sayings such as "come out from among them, and be ye separate…and touch not the unclean thing" (2 Corinthians 6:17 KJV) and "abstain from all appearance of evil" (1 Thessalonians 5:22 KJV) were constantly being employed to justify a separatist lifestyle. Little did I know that these verses were being quoted out of context and that the three little monkeys were speaking for Confucius and not the Bible. In fact, Jesus taught that it was not what goes *into* someone that defiles them, but what comes out, because what comes out comes from a heart that is deceitful and desperately wicked. I believe now that the power of these pharisaical controls are hard to resist. We will always gravitate to an easily defined external spirituality rather than to a more ambiguous, internal judgment that makes us all personally responsible for our own decisions and conclusions. I still feel this struggle today. I still squirm when a Christian college student responds to a talk I give on personal responsibility in cultural matters by the inevitable question: "But where do you draw the line?" A separate world is an easier world. It places more responsibility on others to come up with what is acceptable and what is not. It's also a safer world.

A Safer World

Many Christians today who continue to hold to an extreme doctrine of separation have found a new ally in a multitude of things "Christian" that have been wrestled from the world and made "safe" through a Christian industry that markets to their specific desires and needs. A proliferation of Christian goods and services has resulted, making it possible for Christians to think that by buying Christian rather than worldly goods and services, they are separate from the world.

On the surface, this cultural separation masks itself as a form of godliness, but a closer look reveals an enterprise driven more by self-preservation than anything else. "We may bemoan a moral decline in the country. Our actual concern, if truth be known, is not to see a vital Christianity flourish, but rather to secure a more orderly and less violent society in which to live out our comfortable and self-satis-fied lives."[1] In other words, we want a safer world. We are not as concerned about the salvation of those in the world as much as we want them to behave better around us for our comfort.

This is where so much of our current attitude and approach to the world differs from God's will as expressed in the prayer of Jesus. We want to be safe in a safer world; God wants us safe in an unsafe world. We want to protect ourselves by removing ourselves from danger; God wants to protect us in the middle of danger. These differences may seem insignificant on the surface, but in fact they are huge, involving entirely different worldviews and ramifications.

This theory of safety through removing ourselves from the world could be one of the most dangerous doctrines to invade the church in recent years. It is now thought to be more spiritual to be safe from the world than to interact with it. A separatist Christian monologue has replaced meaningful dialogue with the world around us. Our influence on culture often relies more on some kind of pressure from without—boycotts, marches, and political legislation—than on any kind of friendly presence from within. The high road of involvement, interaction, and mutual respect for those in the world has been abandoned in favor of the low road of disengagement, isolation, and scorn. Thousands of Christians lobby for conservative legislation; few go into politics. Thousands of Christians protest abortion clinics; few provide for single moms or adopt babies. Thousands boycott blasphemous movies; few seek a vocation in Hollywood.

Instead of engaging our culture in a meaningful way, we have often preferred a siege mentality, retreating into the safety of our Christian subculture. We are more comfortable fighting culture than we are being constructively involved in it. Ironically, on every front we mount highly charged rhetorical battles with a worldly culture, while at the same time, within the walls of our subculture, we try to imitate the worldly culture's nuance.

This retreat from the world turns into a sort of cultural catch-22. The more we remove ourselves from the world, the worse the world gets in the absence of a Christian influence and the stronger the argument becomes to stay away from the world. If we were training our children to understand and critically examine the world's popular art, literature, music, and film instead of limiting them to safe Christian versions of these things, we might have a different world waiting for us in the next generation. But it may not be too late for us to rethink our approach.

Undermining the Prayer of Jesus

In this Christian subculture, where safety and protection are seen as being of utmost importance, the prayer of Jesus can be heard as a challenge to our cherished thinking. We have nullified part of what he prayed on our behalf. What's the good of praying for our protection when we have already removed ourselves from the danger? One could even build an argument that the Christian subculture we have created is the result of, at best, a kind of gullible disobedience. We don't like the world we have, and we don't want to be in it, so why not create one we like better? And so everyone follows along with their checkbooks, without really thinking it through.

It's understandable that we would want to protect ourselves and our children from the world, given the nature of the world's dangers, but Jesus prayed for this already. The assumption is that he has more important things for us to do in the world than worrying about keeping ourselves safe from it. Christ's prayer not to take us out of the world but to protect us in it should make us think twice about dedicating so much time and energy to building an alternative Christian subculture. Could it be that God is not against the world after all, at least not in the way we've usually thought?

If we take Jesus' prayer seriously, then removing ourselves from the world undermines the will of God and the prayer of Jesus. The extent to which we have removed ourselves from the world for the sake of safety is the extent to which we may be missing the provision of God in the midst of danger as well as the mission of God in leaving us here in the first place.

Jesus never put walls around himself. He walked openly and fearlessly among the sick, the sinners, the social outcasts, and all those who bitterly opposed everything he did and said. Jesus was vulnerable at all times and relied, as we must also, on his Father for protection. In public, he was almost always among enemies. On numerous occasions he narrowly escaped death at the hands of Pharisees or the riotous crowds they incited. He knew it was not his time. Compare his existence in the world with ours, in contemporary America, and note how carefully we have removed ourselves from danger. We are upset if we have to endure a dirty joke or swearing, as if our righteousness is offended by having to be in the proximity of such behavior.

Jesus did not form an alternative culture with his disciples and set them up against the world. He chose 12 men and then took them with him into the world. He took them into the marketplace and into the homes of strangers. He sent them out as sheep among wolves. He did not come, as some had hoped, to bring a political kingdom. He talked about a kingdom to come, but he taught that the kingdom was within them. He even recognized that his followers were going to have to learn allegiance to both kingdoms at the same time ("Render therefore unto Caesar the things which are Caesar's; and unto God the things that are God's" [Matthew 22:21 KJV]).

He called them to a fearless faith—a faith that had no earthly home and no cultural identity.

Moses, Pointing

I am ashamed, I must admit, that there is not more danger in my own life. Sometimes I feel a little like Moses when he looked across the Jordan and told a murmuring, bickering crowd of Israelites that they should be on the other side of the river where all the giants and the adventures were when he had yet to cross over himself. Some of the concerns I'll raise in these pages come from a dissatisfaction with my own choices—choices that in some ways I cannot alter. Indeed, the very subculture I am questioning in this book most likely put the book in your hands. I certainly have not personally resolved all the issues I raise herein. I'm still learning what it means to be fearless in my faith.

Though I write strongly at times, I am aware that I am biting the hand that feeds me. I would like to claim for myself abandonment to the truth at all costs—to think of myself as John the Baptist in the wilderness—but I am not. I am more like Moses, pointing.

I write of what I know, but not always of what I have experienced. There are others who are further along than I, and chances are they would not bother to speak out about a fearless faith because they are too involved in having one. Sometimes I wonder if this is not the kind of hypocrisy that haunts all writers. We write of what we are searching for more than of what we have embraced and know fully. If we knew it, we would do it, not bother writing about it. Our writing is our reaching out.

That is why I am including in this book the comments of others who have proved themselves to be more fearless than I am. I respect their example. I want their voices to be heard.

A Fearless Faith

We all need to think through why we are here and what our faith is for. By its very nature, faith is dangerous. It puts us at risk in a world at odds with the One we follow and stretches us constantly by the demands it puts on us. And yet there is a glory and an excitement to the risks of faith. We often wonder what motivates those who attempt dangerous feats—competitors in the extreme sports or the Evel

Knievels of today. Maybe it's because there is something built into all of us that embraces risk. We can meet danger with either fear or excitement. When fear rules, it's because deep down we don't believe we have what it takes to face the danger. Excitement comes from knowing and believing that we do.

A fearless faith, then, is one that takes full advantage of the prayer of Jesus. A fearless faith is a faith that is not driven by comfort, safety, and security. It is a faith not necessarily shared by our companions, a faith that thrives in spiritually unfamiliar or even hostile territory, a faith that takes mental discernment to maintain, a faith that is vulnerable and unprotected even weak without the prayer of Jesus to strengthen it and give it courage. A fearless faith does not need a subcultural identity to thrive, for it thrives and flourishes in the heart of the believer.

Real faith is always at risk; the risk is part of what makes it real.

Or as Jesus said in his prayer: "As you sent me into the world, I have sent them into the world." The world was not a safe place for Jesus. Why would we think it would be any different for us?

concepts, probably before most Christians have. The thing that puts us at variance with the larger culture is little more than the fact that we create, sell, and consume our own stuff. We like to stage this as a war of values, but in truth it's a war of partiality, where the values stay pretty much the same. In truth, our values are not that different from the world's.

It may be our stuff versus their stuff, but it's still stuff and the industries that market it. People were appalled when large conglomerates in the entertainment field such as Warner Brothers and ABC bought out smaller Christian music companies such as Word and Sparrow. But it shouldn't be that hard to understand. Whether the content is Jesus or sex and drugs, the businesses are the same. They run on the same principles, follow the same strategies, track the same bottom line.

The Christian subculture is not a location or a community as much as it is a mind-set—a way of thinking. The thinking goes like this: The larger culture is full of sex and drugs, violence and mayhem, godlessness and rebellion. In short, the world is not a place that is conducive to building a life of faith and morality. It is driven by an anti-Christian worldview that controls the major influences in popular culture, including music, movies, television, books, magazines, video games, amusement parks, Web sites, and other forms of culture. Of course, Christians do participate in and enjoy these things, albeit with some degree of guilt. The underlying premise of the Christian subculture is that Christian versions of all that is attractive in popular culture provide a safe, guilt-free means of enjoying them, while building one's faith in the process.

"Beyond books, Bibles and music," the *USA Today* article continues, "they [Christian bookstores] sell clothes, art, jewelry, toys, lap rugs and birdhouses—almost anything to support, proclaim, enhance, deepen or simply decorate beliefs." "Spiritual microclimates" is a term *USA Today* used to describe the evangelical niche that markets to 88 million believers. The microclimate is hot and getting hotter.

"For decades, society was taught to segregate the spiritual from the rest of life," says one leader of the Christian Booksellers Association, which sponsored the trade show covered in this feature article. "It [the spiritual] was looked at as unsophisticated and irrelevant to daily living. Today, people are waking up and saying, 'I am a total person, and there is a spiritual dimension to my life.'"

What this spokesperson failed to see, however, is that segregation is still there. It's just that now a whole subculture has been segregated from the rest of the world. And in subtle and seductive ways, the newer form of segregation is worse than the former. It is worse because it cloaks, under a Christian label, many things that have nothing to do with authentic faith. It placates Christians with assurances of safety and protection, while a great deal that is morally ambiguous slips by undetected beneath the cloak of Christian legitimacy.

Dorky No More

Christians used to separate themselves by their habits and beliefs and their taboos in matters of dress. They not only believed differently from the world around them, but they also looked different and did different things. Christians used to be culturally "dorky" because they were removed from the major cultural influences of the day. Now Christians are no longer dorky. A Christian subculture has now emerged that is much more sophisticated. It looks just like the world except for its content.

Where once Christians felt a personal responsibility to set themselves apart from the world in some visible way, now a subculture does this for us by baptizing our consumption under the name "Christian." The fact that this Christian subculture looks every bit as attractive as the rest of the world makes Christianity that much easier to sell. Bringing the spiritual dimension into harmony with the rest of our lives— something that should be the privilege and duty of every Christian—is now deemed the responsibility of a Christian industry. Why think like a Christian when there are plenty of Christian products to think for you? Why witness when your T-shirt does it for you? Why learn to be critical of culture when you can safely surround yourself with a sanitized Christian version of everything in the world?

It's impossible to read through the comments of sellers and buyers of Christian goods and not sense this have-your-cake-and-eat-it-too rationale. Only in this case it's more like *have all the things you like about popular culture wedded to your Christian beliefs with all the bad things taken out so that you can be cool and be entertained and receive a spiritual bonus on top of that.*

Not that we should go back to being dorky. The issue is much deeper than appearances. The problem from the start has been our tendency to link our identity to external things—dress, language, and cultural taboos. I can think of instances where a committed Christian might swear, smoke, and enjoy a Heineken, while a Christian abstaining from all these things may nonetheless be filled with hatred and sin. We may look like the world, we may look different—neither is significant to the real issues of belief, which we all know lie in the heart.

Cultural Cannibalism

While *USA Today* called the Christian subculture a "spiritual microclimate," an important recent book has dubbed it a "media commune."

In *The 500 Year Delta*,[1] one of the first books to talk about the vast changes facing society at the beginning of a new millennium, marketing gurus Jim Taylor and Watts Wacker organize the current splintering of the social, political, and economic organization of society into what they call "media communes." They uncovered these communes by studying the magazine buying tastes of consumers. What they found in the process was that attitudes and habits within the seven groups they identified could be predicted with remarkable precision. Within the communes are groups they named "Seven Sisters" (female magazines), "Real Guys" (male magazines), "Intelligentsia" (science and economics), and "Armchair Adventurers" (sports and outdoor enthusiasts). One of the seven was a group they called "God Talk." You guessed it—they found a Christian "media commune." This Christian group was, in the authors' words, "the newest of the media communes....This is both the most tightly bound of all media communes—the one most informed by an us-against-them mentality—and the most diffuse."

I suppose you could say it's nice to be recognized in a mainstream cultural analysis, but on the other hand, I'm not so sure this is the kind of attention we want. In this case, being a Christian makes you one of seven marketing targets, not an identity that Jesus had in mind when he formed his kingdom on earth. In other words we are differentiated from the rest of society, not by our faith, but by our tastes, values, and buying habits.

Numerous questions come to mind as we contemplate this new classification of Christians as both a social division and an economic community. How can we expect to have any authority to speak to the rest of society when society has relegated us to a corner all by ourselves? How can our faith and position as representatives of the kingdom of God be taken seriously when we have traded them for a bit part in the political and social dramas of human institutions?

The world has gotten our number and is now getting rich off marketing, to our niche in society, Christianity's beliefs, values, and political agendas. Yes, the world is now marketing us to ourselves—a kind of cultural cannibalism—and picking up the profits along the way. "Live by the sword; die by the sword"—only in this case the sword is media power, not God's power. We've tried to play the world's game and have been outfoxed by a much smarter player.

The most obvious example of this would be the takeover, by secular conglomerates, of the major Christian record companies. Impressed that there is indeed a growing market for value-oriented Christian music, companies such as ABC, Warner, and EMI have simply cashed in on the action. But another indication of what I mean is something I discovered recently on a transcontinental road trip.

Truck World Family Restaurant

In four days I managed to traverse California, Arizona, New Mexico, Texas, Oklahoma, Missouri, Illinois, Indiana, Ohio, and Pennsylvania. I don't know why I like these long drives; I have made this trip four times now, and for three of them I did it solo. Maybe it's the solitude, the time to think, the time not to think, the open road, the sense of space. Admittedly, there are not many observations I have a right to make on such a quick route across the country, but I couldn't help noticing one thing—a significant change in the nature of truck stops.

The last time I made a similar trip was roughly ten years ago. Then, truck stops were pretty grimy places: dusty auto and truck goods and accessories stacked haphazardly on sparsely filled shelves, adult magazines at the checkout counter, an eating area where a waitress would assault you with greasy food and rotgut coffee, dirty bathrooms with dispensers of exotic condoms, and showers you could not imagine getting clean in. Kind of went along with my tough-guy image of truckers.

Well, welcome to Truck World Family Restaurant—an oxymoron at best—where you can get a rag doll, a homey wall plaque, a doggie T-shirt featuring your favorite breed of pooch, a gingham-wrapped box of peanut brittle, or a cute stuffed animal to take home to your kids. Wholesome family videos have replaced the R-rated fare. Christian historical fiction on tape has replaced audio horror novels by Stephen King and Anne Rice. Racks of Christian books are prominent. The ladies behind the counter are all grandmothers in uniformed shirts. I overheard one of them say "God bless you," as she rang the register. A roomy buffet dining room with cheery hostesses awaits you. The bathroom door has a chart on it to record hourly checks for cleanliness, and cologne dispensers are the only vending machines one finds there. Guys with tattoos actually smelled sweet as I passed them in the door. It almost seemed like some kind of Christian takeover of the trucking world by the grandmothers of America. Truck World bite that characteristically accompanies his music. It was "almost" but "not quite."

As a person who has been around for all of Mr. Browne's career, I suddenly felt cheated, as if someone had gotten away with something only because a sound had been buried long enough for its origin to go undetected by a new generation of listeners. Within minutes of hearing this CD, I found myself searching through my old tapes for some real Jackson Browne. I couldn't help it. Suddenly I had this insatiable desire to sink my teeth into the real McCoy, as if somehow I had to assure myself of the integrity of the original source of this sound.

I wonder: How many times does our Christian version of the world recall the original on which it is based? When the world encounters Christians today speaking from the platform of a subculture, does the question "Where have I heard this before?" ever turn up in their minds? All too often, people *have* heard it somewhere, because that is primarily what we have done so far—copied the world for our material. What this means is that the message we're delivering in this process could easily undermine the message we really want to communicate. We might think we're saying something about God or the gospel, but the world is hearing only: "I just wanna be like Jackson Browne."

Song On the Radio

The mix is so wet, it seems to splash out of my radio onto the dashboard of the rental car I am driving. I check my knees for signs of moisture. The gear-shift knob does feel a little damp. The drummer's side-stick echoes all the way to Sioux Falls. The synthetic bass has an edge to it that I can feel somewhere in the lower regions of my stomach, and the kick drum hits me lower still. And then a groaning, twisting female voice wraps itself around the studio microphone, which, through the magic of modern technology and car audio, is now my ear. I hear every crackle inside the singer's mouth, and my heart beats with every breath she takes, and she takes quite a few—more than are necessary to sing this song, I'm sure.

What is this? The sound track to *Dirty Dancing II?* No. This is contemporary Christian music, and I am supposed to assume it is God's love that she is singing about, since this is a Christian station. Unfortunately, in spite of the context, God's love is not the first thing that comes to mind or even the last.

Now, this song would make perfect sense as a pop song on commercial radio. It could even be sung in that arena by an artist who happens to be a Christian. But on Christian radio, a song such as this seems confusing at best. I'm trying to think of whom this song is for, and I'm having a hard time coming up with an answer. If it's to encourage the Christian listener, it's hard to figure out what is being encouraged. The strong sexual overtones make it seem quite inappropriate as an expression of God's love. Nor is there anything in the lyrics that is particularly definitive about God other than the general concept of love. If the song is meant to grab the attention of the non-Christian, then what is it doing on Christian radio? And even if it does happen to grab the attention of a station-surfing non-Christian, I doubt that the love of God would be the obvious interpretation of the lyrics. I'm still trying to find God in this song, and I'm a believer.

The best I can come up with is that this song is for the singer, the record company, and the Christian market. It's for the singer, who wants to sound like somebody, look like somebody, and be somebody, and for the record company, which wants to make money off of all the people who think the singer *is* somebody—but a safer somebody than the somebody else who is the real somebody. After a while, this setup starts to resemble a cultural playground where we get to be like the world without the price, the competition, or the danger. I have a hard time imagining that Jesus Christ is praying that this whole enterprise will be protected from the evil one. Actually, I need him to be praying for me right now while this woman breathes in my ear about "God's love."

Admittedly, I'm making a lot of only one song, but it's because I believe the conclusions I am getting to are true for much more than one particular song. How much of this could apply to the entire enterprise of the Christian marketing of our culture? How much of the motivation behind Christian cultural enterprises is driven and ruled by the same values that grease the wheels of pop culture? Is the only difference that ours is Christian and theirs is not?

Playing World

Baby boomers such as myself (young adults in the '60s and '70s) were the first generation to be heavily influenced by pop culture. Television was introduced during our childhood. Rock and roll was born in our adolescence. Pop culture became our identity. Once we were saved, our faith, in order to be real and meaningful to us, required either a connection to that culture or a complete shunning of it. Most opted to connect. Rock and roll had become our identity, so we claimed Christian rock as unique to ourselves and our times. Television had molded us, so Christian television would mold our children. We started our kids on *Sesame Street* until *Veggie Tales* came along.

Almost too gradually to notice, we were creating a different world for our children and their children after them. Our children have grown up in a world where these cultural connections have already been made for them. While we made up songs for the purpose of speaking to our culture, our children grew up in a subculture based on the marketing and proliferation of similar songs among people who already believe them. What was for us a mission and a message is for them a choice of entertainment between two different cultures—secular or Christian. Where one generation may have engaged culture, the next has embraced a subculture that grew out of that attempt. In essence, Christians under 30 have grown up in, and continue to face, not one, but two worlds. Though this seems like a minor distinction, its ramifications on faith and worldview have been huge.

Now, instead of connecting to and engaging in the worldly culture in which we all live, believers are more likely to run away into the safe arms of a totally Christian world. Instead of cultivating a fearless faith in a dangerous world, Christians are now encouraged to shield a fragile faith in a safe world, and the latter state is worse than the former.

Instead of engaging with a godless culture, we are engulfed in a guarded subculture. Instead of being awake to a challenging world, we are, many of us, asleep in an innocuous alternative world where faith doesn't have to be tested by opposition. Instead of worldly discretion, we have wholesale indiscretion in a subculture that is supposedly safe from cultural toxicity but is perilously infected with it.

This is our world, then, where the sexual overtones of a song on Christian radio seduce the Christian listener into indiscriminately swallowing whole a culture that few on this side of the church are critiquing. Many are not even aware a seduction exists.

Who Really Won?

The shift has been gradual and hard to grasp, but a 30-year perspective shows a major change in our alignment with the world: from persuading to imitating, from engaging to emulating, from influencing to being infatuated. We now are trying to be like the world we once sought to win.

The songs of the early Jesus Movement were attempts to speak to another culture from a counterculture perspective. Over a few short years, however, the songs turned into records, the records turned into record companies, the record companies turned into conglomerates, the conglomerates turned into marketing machines, and one of those marketing machines found this hot female singer who is now breathing seductively on my radio. And no one really seems to care what she's singing as long as the machine is getting greased and lots of people who run the companies and answer the phones and call the bookstores and book the artists and manage the tours and haul the equipment and drive the buses and find the songs and record the songs and play on the recordings are all going to the bank and feeding their families. It's a good thing to feed your family. Especially when you consider that lots of Christian families are happy to now have music that is safe to play for their children, because the world is not a safe place.

Somewhere by the end of the day, it all boils down to our version of culture versus theirs—a very low-impact model when it comes to our influence in the world.

Identity Gap

A discrepancy may exist between what we think we are saying and what people are actually hearing. Likewise, the Jackson Browne soundalike may not even know he sounds like Jackson Browne. He might have heard a sound somewhere in his dad's record collection and liked it. His producer might have been older and thought, *This guy sounds like Jackson Browne. We could produce this record with the same sound.* Similarly, the girl on the radio may be singing to the Lord with all her heart, but I'm interpreting something else entirely. This discrepancy could be called an identity gap. We all have this in our personal lives in some way. How we perceive ourselves is rarely how we are being perceived. I might get angry with my children, feeling entirely justified in my anger, while all they see is my face getting red and veins popping out all over. That might make them laugh because it's so out of character for me. Of course, their laughter would make me even more upset. I might feel they are disrespecting me when in actuality they simply can't help themselves. I look funny to them when I'm angry. For me to not understand this is for me to go on in my anger, adding disrespect to the list of things I hold against them.

In similar ways, Christians have an identity gap with the world. We see ourselves as one thing, but I surmise the world sees us as another. These discrepancies may lead to much misunderstanding between us. If we are ever going to take our faith outside the confines of this subculture, we need to get acquainted with some of these misperceptions.

We need to look at ourselves. What do we look like to the rest of the world? What do we have to overcome to get our real point across to this audience?

Duplicating the World

Let's give this a try. An article in the *Los Angeles Times* about a growing megachurch in Southern California might be a good place to start. Scott Thumma, a professor with Hartford Seminary's Institute for Religion Research in Connecticut, says that the current trend in megachurches is to "create a whole alternative environment for [church] members where they walk into a garden of paradise of sorts. They're taking everyday life and saying, 'We can duplicate it here.' Schools, restaurants, after-school activities—they are duplicating and baptizing everyday life."[1]

This may sound really cool to Christians, but I wonder what the surrounding community thinks about a 500,000-square-foot "garden of paradise" moving into their neighborhood. Don't you think someone might wonder why the church needs a coffee bar when Starbucks is already around the corner? Do non-Christian neighbors really think a church with a gymnasium, coffeehouse, food court, library, bookstore, and rock-climbing wall is for them, or for the comfort and security of its members, whom they see as invading their community?

What sort of message does a megachurch complex such as this give to a community? How much of this $100 million expenditure, under the guise of "outreach," is really just a form of "inreach"? I imagine some might wonder if that $100 million could have been better spent on the local community or the needy. I know the argument from the church would be that all this new stuff is intended to help attract non-Christians. But statistics have proved that the growth of megachurches is always accompanied by a shrinking of attendance in other nearby Christian churches. There are never enough new converts to explain the rapid growth. Christians are leaving smaller churches and going to the big churches because they have better stuff. Much of the world will not be that interested in what is happening. They will just see "those Christians" doing whatever they are doing "over there," but not have enough curiosity to check it out.

At some point we are going to have to answer the question of whether the church should be distinctively different from the culture. Sooner or later this passion we have for relevancy is going to start working against us. Fads are always on a pendulum swing anyway. Non-Christians are going to come to church expecting something different from the world and be disappointed to find a rerun of *Saturday Night Live*.

This change is already occurring among Gen-Xers and younger people. I have been to their services and found a dissatisfaction with what they call the "yuppie church" and a growing desire for an experiential element in worship. Proponents of church-growth programs should think twice before they invest hundreds of millions of dollars into what to the next generation will look more like an overgrown theme park than a church. Perhaps the next generation will want an environment that is clearly religious: candles, religious icons, liturgy, common prayers, and silence. By many indications, these are the marks of the new young church. It doesn't want everything spelled out. It wants mystery. It wants something that is unquestionably a religious experience. Look for architecture to become important again. I wouldn't be surprised if cathedrals make a comeback and visual art plays a predominant role in the new church.

A Xerox Culture

What is this Christian subculture for, anyway? Is it a place where we can simulate the world for our own safety and convenience? Is it a place where well-known Christians can play celebrity—drive around in limos, wear nice clothes, and insist on detailed menus of gourmet food in the dressings rooms of churches where they are performing?

If anything, this duplicating of the world says a lot about how enamored we are with the world. We want to sound like the world sounds, look like the world looks, do what the world does, and be famous like people in the world are famous. If we really want these things, we should go after them legitimately on the level playing field of the wider culture so that our actions and achievements will have more integrity. As it is, we have created our own world with its own version of the rich and the famous.

You can track it like clockwork. Any new fad in the wider culture will have a counterpart in the Christian subculture in due time. Boy bands, girl bands, sexy teen stars, diet plans, aerobics. The only potential change to this well-developed pattern is the shortening of the time it takes for the "Christian version" to appear.

What sort of dent is being made in the wider culture if we act in this manner? What sort of mark are we making on the world by copying it? How can we address the real needs of a culture when we are spending so much time, energy, and money trying to imitate it? How dangerous is it to relate to Christians? You won't find a nicer, more tolerant group of people. It takes a fearless faith to live as a Christian in front of hostile, or even disinterested, unbelievers who give you no points for your faith. But to make your mark in our subculture is no sweat.

"Man in the Middle"

Brooks is a singer and songwriter who mostly plays such venues as clubs, coffeehouses, folk festivals, and house concerts. Though many of his songs are deeply spiritual in nature, they are played, marketed, and sold largely outside the Christian subculture.

The fact that I'm a Christian has a total impact on what I am doing as an artist. When I converted to Christianity in my late teens, I was into music, but I was more into the scene. I was more into the culture. I was more into hanging out and looking cool and having a guitar and playing it loud. It was more about what I was getting out of it—my image, so to speak. But when I converted, music suddenly became the most obvious form of expression. It started out as a natural way to express my gratitude. It just seemed the right thing to do to pick up my guitar and play. I ended up writing the music that came from me naturally without anyone saying, "You know, to be successful you need to do this or that...."

Now I feel passionate about sharing this music on a community level. I'm really interested in the story that all people share. I'm interested in situations that are more universal. What excites me about writing is creating honest pictures of day-to-day life. I like there to be a little element of mystery in the lyrics. But I also like there to be a direction—pointing me somewhere, or reminding me of something, or taking me to another place.

I feel as if I am meant to play the guitar and pursue this music in this way, and I think of that as a very real part of my spiritual journey. Sometimes that's a struggle. There are some days when I am in my music world and I think, "It would be so much easier if I weren't a Christian. I wouldn't have to wrestle with these things, I wouldn't have to be saying to myself, 'Is this what you want to communicate? Is this what you believe? Is this a song you can sing 300 nights a year if you have to?'"

I have been touched so deeply by music, literature, and art that have come from people who aren't Christians, and I have been left feeling so impoverished by a lot of the music, literature, and art that have come from people who are Christians. I don't understand this. It is a mystery that baffles me. When I was younger, I assumed, in my naïveté—my warped, egotistical sense of God and God's rightness—that because I was a Christian, I was going to be the spokesperson for Christianity. I was going to go out and be the most articulate. I was going to sell the most records. I had all these crazy attitudes that had nothing to do with that vague mystery of what touches people's souls and what actually communicates truth.

I don't really fit into the Christian world—the Christian culture. Some days it's a very disconcerting feeling. Sometimes I wish I fit in better with mainstream Christian culture, because there'd be lots of people there to support my music. It would be easier, to a certain extent. Or, on the other hand, if I totally conformed to mainstream culture, it might be easier there. But I'm neither. I'm in the middle, so I live with that wandering, unsettled sense that perhaps all of us feel in the midst of our spiritual journey. But I feel compelled to do exactly what I am doing.

—Brooks

broad Christian market primarily because the broad Christian market did not understand him. His songs have a depth and a raw reality to them that distinguish them from the more predictable, answer-oriented, uplifting pop songs that seem to characterize most of what Christians seem to want to hear. Since his untimely death in 1992, Mark's songs continue to characterize a fearless faith—a faith that goes where not all questions are answered and not all problems are solved.

Read his lyrics again and try to determine what they mean. I don't fully grasp them, yet each time I read them, especially when I hear them sung (for Mark doesn't "sing" this song, he screams it from some dark hole in everyone's human existence), I get something more—something I didn't see the last time. This is a sign of good writing. It challenges us to work harder, dig deeper.

So much of what is Christian these days is simple, direct, and easily swallowed. Lyrics stay on the surface of things. Popular musicians have learned that if your audience can't get a song the first or second time through, the song will probably not find an audience. Though his songs have been recorded by numerous Christian and secular artists and acclaimed by independent critics as brilliant, Mark never achieved much of a following for this very reason. His own words probably say it best: "I'm too sacred for the sinners and the saints wish I would leave."[2]

Safe Radio

In another instance, I recall a talk show host on Christian radio who lost his job because, according to management, he was too well-informed and too intelligent for a Christian audience. It was a blatant admission of their calculated "dumbing down."

Apparently, his show, which included discussions of many elements of pop culture, including books, music, movies, and television, did not have enough appeal to an audience that, in the station's estimation, wanted more policy-driven talk related to right-to-life issues and the latest news coming out of Washington. It seems that too few Christians were interested in staying on track with the host's thought-provoking guests and philosophical reviews. Christian radio is a small-niche format to begin with, and the number of Christians who want to be intellectually challenged, the station believed, is even smaller.

I remember how sad and disappointed I was when I first heard this news. This man's show—a rare voice in Christian radio—had been an island of promise in a sea of predictability, and I couldn't believe we were losing such a bright, thinking Christian from such a place of influence. It was even sadder to think it was mostly due to economic concerns. His was a show that helped Christians see all sides of a conflict rather than focusing on only one aspect of a complex argument. He made his listeners think and question their assumptions—an exercise valuable to the cementing of one's beliefs and the creating of a meaningful dialogue with the world. Why not at least once give people what they may *not* want, but desperately need? Do we have to always sink to the bottom line? Do we have to go to the shallow water because that's where all the fish are? If the bottom line is profit, then we do; and in business, that's the only line there is.

This was clearly a situation where no one seemed fearless enough to take a risk. It was dangerous to keep such a show as this on Christian syndication. There is a political and cultural stereotype that fits the average Christian listener, and this show simply did not match that description. The safe road eventually won out, and the stereotype remained unchallenged.

Sometimes I wonder if Christians aren't a lot smarter than this. What if Christians are actually smarter than the market? What if the "broad Christian market" is self-perpetuating and what it's perpetuating is a lie? Suppose the market feeds that image, which feeds the market, which feeds the image so many times around that the cart gets separated from the horse. What if there are Christians out there, lots of them, who want more intelligent dialogue on lots of issues, but they only hear what this merry-go-round marketing thinks they want, so they eventually tune out, and the ones who remain are the ones who will simply go on listening to whatever the station plays?

The mass media always move toward the lowest common denominator, but does that mean the Christian media have to follow after? It seems that most news and information services are headed for the level of the tabloid market. But does that mean Christian talk show hosts have to dumb down to guarantee a large enough listening audience to keep a show on the air? Are Christians really this disinterested in thinking critically about culture? Or have thinking Christians simply been driven away from Christian radio?

Perhaps Christians are smarter than the broad Christian market. Maybe the broad Christian market is something like the broad way that Jesus said is so crowded with travelers, and maybe the narrow way is just as narrow as it always was, and just as sparsely traveled. If all that glitters is not gold, then perhaps all that glows is not Christian.

More at Stake

There is much more at stake here than just a radio show. Among other things there is our witness to the world. Let's consider the implications...

Radio is a place where non-Christians at least have a chance to overhear our conversation as Christians. They find out what is important to us. But what do they hear us talking about? Do they hear us honestly discussing the questions of faith against the backdrop of our daily human experiences? Do they hear us making intelligent assessments of contemporary ideas? Or do they hear us merely rehashing already well-worn and well-known cultural values and vendettas—the "Christian social issues" of our day? Shouldn't non-Christians be able to hear Christians talking among themselves and at least admire the discussion, even if they do not agree with the assumptions or conclusions?

In his book *A Severe Mercy*, Sheldon Vanauken, a friend and contemporary of C. S. Lewis, tells the story of how a number of erudite Christian friends finally convinced his young wife, Davy, and him to take Christianity seriously. While still unbelievers, they met up with a group of these Christians at Oxford University, Christians who mounted a strong challenge to their preconceived notions about Christianity. Vanauken described how he and his new wife found themselves—surprisingly—fascinated with the discussions they had with these Christian students about the same books, music, and philosophies they were interested in. In describing the process Vanauken writes: "These were our first friends. Close friends. More to the point, perhaps, all five were keen, deeply committed Christians. But we liked them so we forgave them for it....Moreover, the astonishing

with pop songs, advertisements, and TV shows to distract us, and with a Christian subculture to do our thinking for us and even give us reasons for why our brains don't have to work very hard. But learning to employ our minds in the activity of thinking about God all the time can be one of our primary delights as Christians. It is not one more thing to do; it's the thing you do while doing everything else. But look out: thinking deeply and speaking your faith to your culture can be very dangerous. Daniel and his friends got thrown into the fire for this.

Relevant to What?

It isn't enough just to be relevant. It isn't enough to simply put the gospel message into contemporary sounds and images. As good stewards of the secret things of God, we are also responsible for interpreting the meaning of the message for contemporary life. There is no magic formula for doing this—no sprinkling of popular culture with gospel fairy dust. There is only the hard work of interpreting the meaning of the gospel for our own lives and then translating that meaning outward toward the world. To do this properly, one must be a student of both the gospel and our culture, and I fear that so far we have been too enamored with our culture—and too eager to be enamored with our culture—to study it with any objectivity. If all we've done is make the gospel "relevant," history may show us that we haven't done anything at all.

I am reminded here of Paul's identification with Jews, legalists, and those outside the law that he might win them for Christ. And yet, in his attempt to be relevant to those groups, he clearly did not adopt their limitations. For instance, he became *like* those under the law that he might win those under the law, but he did this without putting himself back under the law again (1 Corinthians 9:20). He knew he was not under the law, but under grace, and yet he could take on the perspective of a legalist to speak to those who were under the law. His identification with people did not go so far as to take on their limitations as much as to understand them and be able to communicate with them. This is a very important distinction. We need to learn to understand our culture without being swallowed up by it.

Two Down

He went to heaven the way he performed most of his concerts, with nothing on his feet. More than anything else, those bare feet symbolized something different about Rich Mullins. They captured his vulnerability and humility and, yes, his rebelliousness too. Rich was never happy being on the side of what the world labels success. In the words of one observer, "He was a man who dodged the flash of a camera bulb to try and show us the light of Christ."

Like the death of Mark Heard, it took the death of Rich Mullins to bring out the depth in Rich's music, and in us. Something in these men transcended fame and popularity and promotion and marketing. They each took their blunt tools forged in brokenness and managed to carve out a work that glowed with a light of its own.

Indeed, Rich Mullins would probably not be very happy about all the attention his death received, given the tens of nameless thousands who die each day for want of food and simple medical care. He would want our attentions to be turned to our awesome God and to those on the planet less fortunate than he.

One of the most significant comments upon Rich's death came from his brother, David, who wrote: "Some people were drawn to him because of the goal of his journey. They had the same goal. Others were drawn to him because they saw in him a sinner who was struggling to sin less. In him they saw the good that could be alongside the wrong that they might see in themselves."[4]

Not bad enough to be sinners nor good enough to be saints, most of us waver somewhere between the glow of our sainthood and the guilt of our sin. Rich and Mark fully embraced the paradox of being both sinner and saint. It is impossible to explain Rich and Mark without under-standing this. The divine in the human—an intermingling of God and man—is the essence of incarnation. It was their understanding of this paradox, among other things, that made the work of Rich and Mark stand out as being on a deeper level than others'.

There are movements afoot in Christian music to make the music more "Christian." This maneuver seeks to sim-plify reality. Put all the good guys over here and the bad guys over there. Draw clear lines of demarcation between the sacred and the secular. Pit Christians against the world, and never the twain shall meet. Warn against being unequally yoked with unbelievers, as if we had the ability to even know how to separate the sheep from the goats before our Lord plans on doing it much less the authority to do so.

While all along our problem is our answer. Rich and Mark answered it, and we're still trying to explain what it was they did. They had it all bound up together—the divine and the human, the sacred and the profane. We are always trying to separate the sacred and the profane, when the whole point of our existence is to express the glorious paradox of having the two bound up together in our lives. This is true grace: that God would visit us, enter our hearts, and have fellowship with us in the midst of our fallenness. Without this incarnation, we have no connection with a fallen world.

This is hard for us to embrace because we want our Christian mass media stars to glow with holy righteousness. We demand that Christian ministry be impeccably pure. We want our guys to look better than their guys. But this can happen only if they lie, and we believe it.

These two men, Rich Mullins and Mark Heard, didn't lie in that way, and those who saw their truth have been enriched and deepened in the process. Is it just a coincidence that these deaths have cut down two men who have told the truth about themselves, who have hurt for a world around them, and given little thought to their success or lack of it? Theirs was a fearless faith, and though on the surface you could say their early deaths were the tragic result of a heart attack and an automobile accident, I have never believed it was that simple or coincidental. I believe these two paid for their faith with their lives.

"Christian Milk from a Christian Cow"

Tony, 36, is a marketing executive for a small record company that specializes in acoustic folk music. Though the record company is in North Carolina, Tony manages to live in the Midwest to be near his extended family. He was a very successful, well-liked promotions director for a major Christian label in Nashville when he quit that job to move to his present location.

I can tell you exactly when I knew I had to leave Christian music. I was in a marketing meeting studying the so-called WWJD phenomenon that had moved large quantities of T-shirts, bracelets, and hats through Christian bookstores nationwide. Our general manager pointed out that this thing was a "multimillion dollar catchphrase." He wanted us to jump on it and come up with the next Christian phrase that would replace it and then market the heck out of it. I knew right then that I could no longer have anything to do with an enterprise that made money off of marketing Jesus to Christians.

Don't get me wrong; these are nice people. Like me, they had all gotten into this business for the right reasons. We wanted to help sincere Christian artists get their message out. But it's a gradual, slippery slope. One little compromise on top of another, and suddenly you're planning how to make lots of money off of Jesus. I take the worship of Christ seriously, and I no longer felt right about being part of a subculture that would sell John 3:16 to Christians for $15.95. It would have been hypocritical for me to stay in this industry once I realized this.

Most of what we ended up creating didn't have artistic integrity. In the '70s it was all grassroots ministry, but by the '80s, big business took over and we started marketing to a subculture. Everything became inbred, self-contained. Christian milk from a Christian cow. By creating a subculture we watered down the message.

We should be presenting ourselves artistically, right on the shelf with everybody else. I work for a company now that's trying to do that. It's hard, and it may not work, but we'll die trying. Either we'll do it right or we won't do it at all. I tell my boss he's way too honest and way too fair to his artists to ever make a living in Christian music.

The church used to be the source of the world's greatest art, but now it has turned its back on that. Now the Christian subculture is where you go to find some of the worst art. Every time we make a movie it's about the end times. And then we market it to ourselves. We already know what's going to happen.

—Tony

CHAPTER SIX

Stereotypical Christianity

---- ✥ ----

Gospel Tipping

Kay is a waitress in Ohio. She's been waiting tables as a steady job now for 11 years. Kay's life has been anything but rosy, although she does refer to a nine-year period when she enjoyed what she calls "that perfect Christian-bubble life." But that bubble of bliss is now only a memory, even though her faith remains strong. Her husband, who ironically had started her on the road that led to Christ, left her with two small children. Now she tries to survive despite being without $11,000 in unpaid child support. Needless to say, Kay works hard at her job and is glad to have Jesus Christ in her life.

Like all waiters and waitresses, Kay notices when people don't leave tips or they undertip her. A server's salary takes tips into account. Every little bit counts. And it's not only the money but an integrity issue as well. A poor tip is taken as an intentional insult for poor service. I know of a waitress who will run after a poor tipper with his measly offering in her hand and say, "Here, you can have this back. You obviously need it more than I do."

So when a table of people recently bought four medium-priced dinners and blessed Kay with a gospel tract and a whole dollar bill inside, Kay failed to see the blessing. It was not the first time such a thing came from a Christian patron. In fact, according to Kay, Christians are notoriously stingy tippers. She is constantly apologizing to her coworkers for the poor example of her fellow Christians.

Christian Caricature

The impression these Christians are leaving on Kay's coworkers is a bad blow to an image already damaged in the world's eyes. Christians have been stereotyped by our culture with a negative image that has little or nothing to do with what our identity should be as genuine followers of Christ. This typecasting has become so prevalent in the media that a Christian has become, in the world's eyes, less of a person and more like a caricature. Sometimes the portrayal is simply mean-spirited and wrong. More often than not, however, it is based on real experience and needs to be something we take seriously. Kay's characterization of Christians as tightfisted and lacking in generosity, for instance, appears to have a good deal of truth in it. After I published an article about Kay in my monthly column, I received numerous reports from waiters and waitresses around the country confirming similar reports of stingy Christians.

Kay and her coworkers especially dread Sundays, when a high percentage of their clientele are Christians enjoying dinner out after church. Apparently this day is famous for having the highest food sales (and thus requiring the hardest work) but the lowest tips. "This speaks a negative message to my coworkers who do not know Christ," she wrote in a letter to Good News Publishing, the maker of the tract the four Christians left her. "I have found that homosexuals and bikers are consistently better tippers than Christians."

That's right, Kay wrote a letter to the organization that made the tract. Not that they bear responsibility for those who use such a tool inappropriately, but Kay was hoping a kind suggestion might be a good place to start helping people who distribute these tracts to think differently about how they live their lives before non-Christians. "I do not know how you package these [gospel tracts] for sale," she wrote, "but I would suggest enclosing a note that reads: 'If the words of this tract are rooted in your heart, then remember to flesh them out as you leave your tip. The generosity of the love of God is not revealed when we grasp and hoard.' "

It remains a mystery to me how we can walk out of church, where God's mercy has been poured out on us, and walk into a restaurant and stiff the first person we meet. It's like the parable that Jesus told of the manager who, having just had his debts canceled by his master, reciprocated by extracting every last cent from those who owed him something (Matthew 18:23-33).

Our actions always speak louder than our words. One of the greatest hindrances to our witnessing is when we shoot ourselves in the foot by our poor behavior among non-Christians. Imagine how much easier it would be for Kay to witness to her co-workers if Sunday were the day they all looked forward to because of the consistent generosity of Christians. As one letter writer put it: "Everything we do as a Christian, with or without a tract involved, says 'Jesus' on it."

Branding

Sometimes I wish we had a new word for "Christian."

I bet there are a lot of people who would be Christians if they didn't have to become a Christian to be one. If that sounds confusing, it's because I'm not talking about true Christianity, but about how the word "Christian" has been translated into contemporary American life and culture. "Christian" has now become commonplace. But what we think of when we use the "C" word is rarely what the world is thinking.

When the average non-Christian hears the word "Christian," he or she doesn't think of the Body of Christ or the church at large or of followers of Christ in all cultures, classes, races, and nationalities. The person is more likely to have in mind a kind of American cultural Christianity that is a composite of what has surfaced in the media in this country in the last 15 to 20 years—a stilted stereotype at best. Whether we like it or not, we have been branded with an image, and the image is not a good one.

An important part of marketing products has to do with consciously branding these products with an image or impression through advertising and corporate sponsorships. For instance, LL Bean has come to represent Yankee honesty and value; Volvo has a worldwide reputation for building the safest cars; Disney is the undisputed expert at entertaining children (of all ages). These associations are no accident. They are designed by marketers to tie a personality or identity to a product or company aimed at a targeted market. Though the Christian brand may not have been the brainchild of a conscious marketing strategy, we are branded nonetheless by a largely negative image, a one-dimensional caricature that is hard to identify with and easy to dismiss. It is an image that most non-Christians would reject, even those who would be Christians were they to encounter true Christianity. In truth, many Christians reject it too, but few non-Christians know this unless they get close enough to our lives to see the difference.

The world hears "Christian" and sees a white, middle-class conservative on a political soapbox with an American flag in one hand and a Bible in the other. The world doesn't imagine a kid with dreadlocks and bones in his nose singing about Jesus. It doesn't imagine an African-American pastor helping neighborhood kids get off drugs. It doesn't think of a body of Vietnamese Christians sharing a church with Hispanic believers in the middle of rural California. And saddest of all, it doesn't see nonjudgmental people with compassion who are marked by their kindness to others and generous spirit of service and unconditional love. It is truly a tragedy that a merciful gospel that welcomes everyone is branded by an image that represents only a few.

We are not blameless in this. Much of this negative branding is the price we are paying for a misplaced faith in questionable political alliances. We thought we could gain back lost cultural ground through political power and influence, when all we did was make enemies of those Christ came to save. For a while there, we got a little carried away with the publicity, because, as the public relations game goes, negative publicity is still publicity. To the extent we believed that is the extent to which we are now stuck with the political backlash that capitalizes on all our worst traits:

legalism, judgmentalism, narrow-mindedness, and bigotry. The Christians currently portrayed on television and in Hollywood do not make many believers proud.

As Christians, we are all bearers of Christ, and our lives become the proving ground of faith in the world. If the world rejects the Christian brand, it may not be such a bad thing as long as authentic Christians give people something tangible to put in its place. That kind of witness can't be found in a song, a television show, or a film series, or even a seeker-sensitive church service. It comes over coffee, or at the ball game, or while carpooling to work or working out at the gym. Personally, I think the world is full of people who would be Christians if they could just meet and get to know a "real" one.

Christians need to be shaken out of these stereotypes as much as the world needs to encounter the Christian message free of them. There is a place for the public representation of a Christian and the Christian point of view, but it will take Christians knowing how to work along with, not against, the dominant influences of culture to create this place.

They'll Know We Are Christians by Our T-shirts

All this bad press has rendered counterproductive any attempt we make to identify ourselves as Christians in the world. To draw attention to our Christian faith, in most circles, is the worst thing we can do to our chances of sharing the gospel.

A gentleman once told me that when he was in public, he used to wear a T-shirt with a clear Christian message on it, hoping it would give him an opportunity to witness for

Christ. It should come as no surprise that no such opportunity ever arose. A Christian T-shirt in this present climate is like a flag of allegiance to a group most non-Christians want to steer clear of. None of the people this man really wants to reach will want to talk to him while he is in that T-shirt.

Then he told me that another T-shirt in his collection, which he had picked up from his local music store, had a Fender logo on the front. Being a guitar player who likes Fender guitars, he was naturally drawn to this shirt. It dawned on him one day that without any conscious effort he had had conversations with three different strangers and one conversation had ended up being about God. On that day, he happened to be wearing his Fender T-shirt. All of the conversations had begun with something related to guitars or music. The conclusion here is pretty obvious: The Fender T-shirt witnesses better than the witnessing T-shirt.

Now of course the T-shirt didn't witness; it was the wearer of the T-shirt who witnessed. The T-shirt merely put the man in a position to have a non-threatening relationship with someone. A Fender guitar player is no threat to society. Guitar players who find each other out in the world are not vying for attention or political clout. They simply have something in common: a love for music, in particular the sound of the guitar. It could have been any number of things that attracted people to identify with the man in the Fender T-shirt: mountain climbing, hiking, running, flying model airplanes, boogie boarding, barbecuing, gardening—I think one can see this is an endless list. There is value, in other words, in having interests outside our Christian faith that connect us with people and make us credible on levels other than our Christian beliefs.

This man's experience should help us learn something about today's society and our need to be wise believers in our interaction with non-Christians. We live in a society fragmented by groups and factions. These factions—whether racial, political, social, or religious—are stereotyped by the media and reduced to a sound bite or an image in the movies, in TV sitcoms, or on the nightly news. In this environment, the Christian T-shirt becomes a brand, a logo, a flag—something that identifies the wearer. No wonder no one wanted to talk to the man in his Christian T-shirt. They saw him as *"one of those Christians,"* a group about which much of society has already formed an unfavorable opinion.

We need to be well-rounded human beings capable of interacting with those around us on a variety of subjects and interests. The most interesting Christians are those who are also interested in living a full life, being well-read, and having a variety of pursuits and experiences, all of which simply create more avenues to meet people and establish relationships.

If we want to have meaningful conversations with people, perhaps seeing our Christianity on our chests, or anywhere else on our bodies for that matter, should not be the first thing about us they encounter. We would be much better off living our Christianity than wearing it, anyway. Maybe we should give all our witnessing stuff to the Salvation Army and dress like everybody else.

We have to be wise enough about our faith to be able to have a conversation about guitars or other interests that may end up as a conversation about Jesus. Not having a T-shirt to do this witnessing for us could be the best thing that ever happened to our faith and our ability to share our faith in a meaningful way and without fear.

American Pie

Bye-bye, Christian culture, bye-bye.
Drove my Ford for the Lord 'till the gas tank went dry.
Them industry types are drinkin' Perrier and lime,
Singin': "This could be the day that I die."

I doubt that contemporary Christianity means much of anything anymore outside the subculture that champions it. There was a time when being contemporary in the realm of faith was the new thing. It was an attention getter on its own. Contemporary faith also used to be considered countercultural. Now being contemporary and part of the popular culture is the norm in the average church. It is expected. Contemporary Christianity is just another demographic on a sales chart, a niche in someone's marketing plan, a bull's-eye on a targeting campaign, a gold mine for a conservative political agenda, a mailing list in someone's data bank. Contemporary Christianity, in short, has been swallowed up by the popular culture.

Bye-bye, gospel pie in the sky.
Drove my Ford for the Lord, but my gas tank went dry.
Now stars in their cars grab a piece of the prize,
And a preacher can cash in on the pie.

Christianity has established such an identification with today's popular culture that it is hard to spot where the Christianity stops and the culture begins, and vice versa. Like a cross that once held a bleeding savior and now is a tattoo on a pop star, the message of sin, guilt, the cross, and the resurrection of Jesus Christ has blended into the cultural landscape to a point where it no longer clashes with anything. Sin is dysfunctional behavior, guilt is a bad feeling, the cross is God's love song to the world, and the Resurrection is merely one more beginning.

Actually, this may not be such a bad thing. It could usher in a fresh opportunity for the gospel. We're going to have to make sense of faith in a world where few can be trusted, and many can be fooled. It's a little like starting all over, and that may not be such a bad thing after all.

Bye-bye, Christian culture, bye-bye.
Drove my Ford for the Lord 'till the gas tank went dry.
But we've a gospel to tell and the truth never lies,
And we're in this 'till the day that we die.

"We're Shallow"

Aaron is 19 years old. He grew up in a Christian home and has been a Christian as long as he can remember. He owes his knowledge and intellectual curiosity to his love for classical literature. In fact, he wants to teach English some day in a public school, using classical literature to point kids toward God and the big issues of life.

It happened for me the first time I read Dostoyevsky's *Crime and Punishment.* I'd never had a novel swallow me up before. But this book was so full of the depths of human depravity, God's grace, and forgiveness that I was awed by its power. Good art says so much that's true about the world.

Christian fiction, on the other hand, presents us with a different kind of world—a safer one. Most of our Christian writing is just another form of preaching. Of course, Christians aren't alone in being preachy. Even non-Christians write propaganda, such as the socialistic bent in some of Steinbeck's works.

The problem lies with our culture. It is lacking in depth, period. Our wealth and our entertainment distract us from dealing with life's weightier issues. Everything of value in life is reduced to one-liners and laugh tracks.

Christians are no different, and this is inexcusable because we have the tools to deal with the real issues. We have not been redeemed by things that corrupt, such as silver and gold, but by the blood of Christ. We should be the ones who can face up to all of life. We should be people of depth. Instead, we're shallow, and our art reflects that.

I just finished a study of the Lincoln-Douglas debates. The debates were six to eight hours long. They included two-hour talks followed by rebuttals full of long, complicated sentences. People listened, followed along, and got riled up. Compare that with our modern presidential debates, which can be reduced to sound bites and effective lighting and makeup.

—Aaron

CHAPTER SEVEN

Against the World

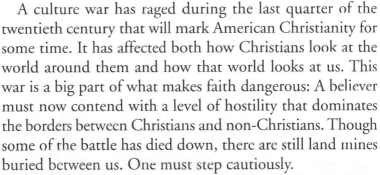

A culture war has raged during the last quarter of the twentieth century that will mark American Christianity for some time. It has affected both how Christians look at the world around them and how that world looks at us. This war is a big part of what makes faith dangerous: A believer must now contend with a level of hostility that dominates the borders between Christians and non-Christians. Though some of the battle has died down, there are still land mines buried between us. One must step cautiously.

Around the time of the Reagan era, moral issues began to play a significant role in politics. Supreme Court decisions had taken prayer out of public schools, Roe vs. Wade had legalized abortion, and gay activists were beginning to clamor for their rights and benefits in society. As Hanna Rosin, religion editor for *The Washington Post* put it, "The average Evangelical was now a Midwestern mother with a Volvo and a degree from a state university furious that her kids could pick up *Heather Has Two Mommies* at the school library and contemplating homeschooling them."[1]

Well, those kids have been homeschooled, the Christian Right has arisen—boosted by a tenacious company of grass-roots Christian activists—and pastors have taken up the banner of politics and morality while their congregations have taken to the streets. Shouts of "Are we going to stand by and do nothing while the secular humanists strip away the moral fiber of this country?" have been answered with a resounding "No!" Christian radio, once a disseminator of the gospel of Jesus Christ has turned into a platform for venting rage against baby-killers, homosexuals, and feminists, and for mobilizing Christians to action. James Dobson turned from focusing on the family to focusing on political issues that affect the family.

And the war has raged. We've seen movies boycotted, abortion clinics bombed, Hollywood studios marched upon, and candidates deified and vilified. Even kid-friendly Walt Disney Studios was boycotted for awarding rights to gay employees, and Moses himself (Charlton Heston) became the president of the National Rifle Association.

Even though things seem to be quieting down somewhat due both to an erosion of support from the Republican Party and the country's general swing toward the middle, there is still a fallout effect from the assault Christians have made on the world. Most of that fallout comes in the form of anger. In simplest terms, Christians are still angry at the world for being so bad, and the world is angry at Christians for thinking Christians are so good.

I have a friend who speaks often in seminars for Christian leaders around the country. In one of his talks he launches into a familiar tirade about how bad the world is, and then, when he's really got his audience worked up, he says, "God must really hate the world." For him, this is just a tactic in his speaking. He's showing his audience that if they aren't thinking, their emotions will lead them to a place far from the truth. He is reminding them that the most famous verse among Evangelicals is the one that tells us how much God loves the world and gave his only Son to save it (John 3:16). But he says he's always shocked, every time he does this, at how easy it is to get Christians to agree that God hates the world and at how angry these Christians become. That can mean only that these Christians must hate the world. There is a strong moral indignation at work in the church that doesn't appear to be going away any time soon.

Of course God doesn't hate the world; we hate the world. And we like to think that God agrees with us, that God is on our side.

With God on Our Side

Bob Dylan wrote the song "With God On Our Side" in the 1960s, and like many of his songs that were socially prophetic, this one foreshadowed a new Christian body politic that would blend Christian morality with a sense of national manifest destiny. Ours was a Christian nation that had strayed far away from its roots. It was time to reclaim the moral high ground. Jerry Falwell's Moral Majority, which had been a silent majority too long, took shape. Soon the Moral Majority became the Christian Coalition, and the untapped grassroots potential of the local church suddenly turned into one of the strongest, most unified political movements since Prohibition.

Dylan sang about hating and fearing our enemies, and about running and hiding out. These are the same negative attitudes that crept into the Christian subculture and turned into an ugly holy war what began as a well-meaning moral and spiritual call to the nation. For the Christian Right, the Russians of Bob Dylan's song were replaced by the secular humanists of the '80s, with the same results. Fear began to dominate the airwaves of Christian radio. Hatred of the enemy (anyone with a liberal agenda) became a motivation for involvement. Now it was us against the world, and the growing hostility on both sides sent Christians running to the safety of a subculture where we could hide, lick our wounds, and regroup for other attacks.

Get Back to Where You Once Belonged

Of utmost concern to those who want to live a fearless faith is the defensive reaction this war has elicited from the world. It's pretty much a given now that the people we want to reach with the good news of Jesus Christ are already mad at us over the bad news for which Christians of today have become famous. If we are going to change this, we will have to think differently about the world and about what our affiliation with politicized solutions can and cannot do.

We Christians in America who were seeking political solutions to a moral vacuum made one of the biggest errors we could make. We assumed we could go back to something that was once true about our country. This assumption is problematic for at least two reasons. First, we cannot be completely sure that our national origins are as Christian and as pure as we like to make them out to be. Historians themselves rewrite history, since history is colored by one's own biases. And even if we are right about our version of history, the world will always counter with its own version.

Second, even if we could go back, it's a different world now, and people think differently than they used to. It would be impossible to get people to go back to something they currently do not have the moral framework to grasp.

The mind-set of the founding fathers, even if they were not Christians, was that there is a Guiding Hand that supports the ideals of truth and freedom in the universe. Such thinking is inaccessible to the postmodern mind. Today, there is no Hand, no God, and no ideal. Even Christians today do not think in terms of the sovereignty of God over secular culture as Christians once did. You cannot replace overnight what took more than 200 years to tear down.

Almost 200 years ago, John Adams, one of America's Founding Fathers and the second president of the United States, stated: "Our Constitution was made only for a moral and religious people. It is wholly inadequate to the government of any other." In other words, our Constitution does not guarantee morality and religion. Such things must come from the people themselves, and if morality and religion are no longer present in the people, there is nothing the government can do to represent this morality and religion. In a democracy, the government can never be any better than its people.

We live in a democracy that supports the rights of the individual to life, liberty, and the pursuit of happiness. If we live in a postmodern society with no spiritual or biblical assumptions or absolutes, then the same democratic system that once supported a Christian moral universe now supports a godless one, not because the government has gone bad and needs to be made right again, but because the people have changed. And if the people have changed, government will never change them back. Nor will boycotts, marches, or any other form of political or social pressure. It's the hearts of the people that need to change.

The moral vacuum in our country is not the fault of America nor is America our hope for improvement. Democracy is merely doing its job, as it always will. There is no "Christian nation" to recapture; there are only the hearts of people that have to change. Politics may change a few laws, but using politics to try and change a heart is like trying to perform heart surgery with a baseball bat.

The true church is the only body in society that deals effectively and eternally with the hearts of people. This is why it is so tragic when Christians resort to political power and economic pressure to force a change on society, a change that can truly come only from a heart that is changed. By so resorting, we abandon our calling and our privilege as living representations of the one true God who provided a way back to himself through the death and resurrection of his one and only son. We become just like any other special interest group in society, such as the National Rifle Association or the National Education Association—one more voice among the many. And in doing so, we alienate ourselves from the very people whose hearts the gospel could change if those people could only hear the gospel above the noise of our shouting. Who is going to want to hear the gospel of Jesus Christ from a group that is forcing its own special interests on them? We are not here, for instance, to stop homosexuals from practicing so that society can be rid of their influence. We are here to bring the gospel to everyone, including homosexuals.

If we think we are ready to throw the first stone at an immoral society, then we had better make sure we are right with ourselves on all accounts. And if we are not free from sin, then we had best let these stones roll out of our hands and get back to preaching a gospel that we as Christians need just as much as the next guy.

America is not a "Christian nation" to be recaptured. It is a democracy still doing what it was supposed to do all along. If John Adams was right, and our Constitution is wholly inadequate to the government of a people who are not moral and religious, then it is imperative that we who know Christ attend to living and proclaiming the message of the gospel, which alone is adequate to reach the hearts of people. Use politics for what politics is useful for. Religion is not one of those things.

> The religious, like everybody else, are tempted by politics. Seduced by its efficiency. By its potential. By the good it can do. And, it must be added, by the sheer delight of being, or believing oneself to be…at the center of things. Who wants to be a voice crying in the wilderness when we can be witnesses testifying before Congress? Who wants to be a prophet without honor in his own land when White House breakfasts are available? Who wants to store up treasures in heaven when there are elections to be won here on earth?
>
> If history has taught us anything, it is that religions that fall too deeply in love with the art of politics lose their souls —very fast.[2]

These words from Yale law professor Stephen L. Carter, in his book *God's Name in Vain,* came a little too late. We have already been seduced. The damage has already been done. The world now sees Christians primarily as moralists out to reform society and take away the rights of unbelievers.

A Subculture in Retreat

Are we? Are we out to reform society? Perhaps our goals were this lofty at the beginning. We might have thought we could actually force a change on society using outside forces. The notion that we could use politics to accomplish moral and spiritual ends has pretty much vanished now. That a known conservative Christian with a track record of sympathy toward the Christian political agenda was sworn in as attorney general of the United States is an indication that cooler minds have prevailed. A bitter fight for his acceptance was to be expected, but those who stuck with him believed he would represent more causes than his own personal ones if those causes represented the wishes of the American people. That John Ashcroft was approved and Robert Bork was not is a sign of declining intimidation. The membership numbers are way down for the Christian Coalition, and Ralph Reed, its smart, young, former leader is now doing independent consulting. There is a new, tempered approach to the world that seems to be less threatening to the opposition.

In another indication of a waning Christian Right, two of the Christian Coalition's strongest supporters, Ed Dobson and Cal Thomas, jumped ship and published a book about the incompatibility of the gospel and American politics. Their book, *Blinded by Might,* agrees with the conclusions of Stephen Carter quoted earlier in this chapter: When you mix politics and the gospel, the gospel always loses. As Christians begin to get smarter about politics and the limits of political solutions, what is going to replace this zeal for political solutions? Will a new complacency set in? Will the last state be worse than the first?

Apocalypse When?

Christians are in a dilemma, anyway, when it comes to politics. Our theology tells us to preach an apocalypse "then," as in the coming judgment. Our politics tell us to preach an apocalypse "now," because of the miserable shape the world is in. So on the one hand our theology explains to us why the world is falling apart and asserts our job is to save as many souls as possible before the end comes. But on the other hand, we have been preaching—since the Jesus Movement and Hal Lindsey's *Late Great Planet Earth*—that the deterioration of society will in fact hasten the coming of Christ. Christians began to be concerned about the world they were living in and wanted to do something about it. And as baby boom Christians grew up and had children, they wanted a better world for their children to grow up in. So hold the Apocalypse.

These two doctrines are in conflict, and taken together, they convey an ambivalence about the world. We're still here, but we're not sure why.

Hanna Rosin explains this dilemma in the following way: "No one has worked out a premillennial action guide for politics. Evangelical leaders remain at heart willfully naive to the principles of prudent politics, such as compromise and deal making, so they wind up frustrated and neurotic, trapped between fatalism and activism." Thus, in her estimation, Christians in politics will continue to be "an angry, disembodied voice, crackling on the radio."[3]

Ultimately, the saving of souls should be of preeminent importance to believers. Even our concern for a safer world should be subservient to this.

Walking Through a Minefield

Christians need to step cautiously when dealing with non-Christians because of these sensibilities. Many feelings are still raw from being rubbed the wrong way by a Christian agenda. We will undoubtedly be prejudged for this. I am not saying that Christians should abandon politics. We are citizens of this democracy, and that citizenship requires more involvement in government than most nations require. It is as much a privilege as a responsibility. What we need to guard against is developing a "Christian political agenda." After all, Christians will not always find themselves in agreement on all the issues, parties, and candidates. Politics is never that clean and simple. In fact, it would actually be good for the world to see us disagree about politics and agree about the gospel. Our primary objective is not to be a force for social change; we are first to be bearers of the gospel of Jesus Christ and carriers of his kindness.

We need to realize that politics can be a danger zone for people of faith. I've heard it said that two topics can always start a fight: politics and religion. If this is true, then mixing them can be lethal. We are dealing with flammable substances here. One need look no further than the history of the nation of Ireland to see the fiery consequences of marrying politics and religion.

Some of us will be more involved in political matters than others will be. We all need to realize the limitations of our political involvement and always defer to our faith, which with the love of Jesus crosses all lines and all barriers.

The Fear Factor

One final point needs to be made in relation to our positioning against the world we inhabit, and that is the predominance of fear in the Christian subculture. Fear is the impetus of much of the negative Christian activity in the world. Fear, which is often simply the other side of anger, sabotages much of the hope that the world should be seeing in us. Fear and anger are both unhealthy, unbiblical reactions to a dangerous situation. They both demonstrate a glaring lack of reliance on Jesus' prayer for our protection. Corner an animal and you will get either anger or fear. Unfortunately, when you corner a Christian you often get the same things.

Take for example the Christian reaction to the Y2K scare. At the end of 1999, it looked to me as if we were much too scared and too focused on earthly preparedness to make any headway in the world as representatives of heaven. Here was a splendid chance to show the reality of Christian hope. And yet what did the world observe? In many ways we were the most frenzied. We sold millions of books and videos to each other about the millennium and funded, by our attendance, hundreds of seminars on Y2K preparedness. There were those among us who capitalized on fear. We panicked in full view of a world that is supposed to see us walking fearlessly in the light. It seems to me that we still have some explaining to do.

Y2K turned out to be only a test, and I for one didn't do so good. I'd like to say my casual approach to it all was because of my faith in Christ, but truthfully, I was comforted more by the overwhelming majority of experts assuring us there would be no problem than I was by Christ.

I have to ask myself: Whose words comforted me more, those of the experts in the media or those of Christ when he said, "Do not let your hearts be troubled. Trust in God; trust also in me" (John 14:1)? It seems I run to the words of Jesus when things get really bad, but until then, the experts will do. I don't think that's living by faith. Here are the questions I must ask myself now: How connected am I to the things of this world? How much does my faith in Christ have to do with what I actually put my trust in? Is my faith as real as my fear? Only then can I truly say I have a fearless faith.

In Larry Norman's famous apocalyptic song "I Wish We'd All Been Ready," his concern is not for himself but for those left behind. The song can function like a dream about Y2K from which we awaken and find we're all still here, but now we see from a new perspective. Dry food and a generator will provide little comfort at the end of the world. Our concern needs to be for others, not just ourselves. Do we really care about their souls?

"Devil Lama?"

Steve Duin is a columnist for the Portland (Oregon) Oregonian.
These comments were excerpted from an article he wrote after the
Dalai Lama visited Portland in May 2001.

So this is how religious wars begin? Just how frightening
and divisive was the Dalai Lama's message? Brace yourself. He
preached empathy and compassion. He suggested that inner
peace is the cornerstone of world peace. He gently blocked the
notion that he, or any other Buddhist monk, is the way toward
truth and life. And repeated the heresy that a good heart is
more valuable than any religion's rituals.

So why were so many Christians up in arms? I can hear the
opening volleys in another insidious holy war. How many is
"many"? That's a fair question. For all I know, the same fruit-
cakes are going about their daily rounds, threatening abortion
providers, nailing the Ten Commandments to the elementary
school door, leaving those acidic anonymous messages on our
religion reporter's voice mail. Did I say "anonymous"? Forgive
me: Most of the nastiest stuff was delivered "in Christ's name."
Whatever the final count, more than enough fundamentalists
took to the streets to damn the Tibetan refugee as an idol-
worshiper or dismiss him as the "Devil Lama." As the Good
Book says, we'll know they are Christians by their love.

While I (regretfully) slept through the Dalai Lama's visit,
everyone I've spoken with who lent him an ear was blown away
by his message and/or his presence.

"What I found so intriguing," said Bill Hamilton, the former
priest who heads up Easter Seals Oregon, "is that he does not
surround himself with the trappings of power. He's simple in his
tastes, the way he dresses, the food he eats. And he's basically

saying we're all on a journey, we're all searching for how to make ourselves better people."

"He's a tried and true symbol of someone who strives to do right without getting in other people's way," says Irvin Levin, the founder of Renaissance Holdings. "If you believe the world isn't safe until everyone believes what you believe, you're going to have a problem with the guy." And too many Christians— or just enough to attract attention—have decided that the way to act on that belief is to draw an unnecessary line and pick an unnecessary fight.

Such righteousness isn't a bad thing when it reigns in the privacy of one's disciplined cell. But it tends to get a little unnerving when it is dragged out into the public square in a conscious attempt to provoke the open warfare so antithetical to the message of the monk. I have no idea to what extent fear (of what? wholesale conversion to Buddhism?), stupidity or the notion that Christians can't catch a break in the public arena inspired the reaction to the Dalai Lama's visit.

"The Dalai Lama made this point over and over again," Levin said: "Being religious doesn't make you virtuous." And the goal of "being virtuous" is a marvelous starting point for anyone's spiritual journey. That's a journey Christians should encourage, regardless of the awkward, grasping form it takes. Because if Christians are right in their conviction that their spiritual food is the last, great supper, and their gospel the best news of all, they should have a little more faith that their cross prevails in the end.

—Steve Duin

CHAPTER EIGHT

The Fundamental Element of Safety

———————— ✺ ————————

I ran a footrace in the second grade for the privilege of walking Jane Parmalee home from school. As far as I can remember, with the exception of going to a bowling alley in the eighth grade on a double date with Meg Flory, Jane was my first and last non-Christian girlfriend. From junior high on, the rest of my dating and social life would revolve around a church youth group and, later, a Christian college.

In a time when peer relationships can mark a child's identity for years to come—perhaps for life—it is common for parents to want to control the environment in which these relationships are established. When I was young, the church was most useful for this. Now many more options are available to Christian parents. Christian schools, homeschools, and a whole line of hip Christian products and entertainment alternatives help foster an environment that is Christian, popular, and most important, safe.

Enter the Christian subculture—an alternative environment to a dangerous world—as protector of our kids. No need for a fearless faith in a place where belief is the acceptable norm—where even if you don't believe, you look like you do. Whatever the factors are that have brought on a Christian subculture in America, one of the driving forces that now justifies it, and keeps it vigorous, is the element of safety.

Rebel Grandma

She grew up Catholic but hardly ever went to church. Her husband used to comment on the cute little Baptist church they passed all the time that was near their home in a small town in Massachusetts. So when he died and she was suddenly alone, she decided to go there one Sunday. As she tells it now, the Holy Spirit told her to go. That first Sunday morning at the Baptist church was when Anna became a Christian. She still attends that church even though she now lives 25 miles away in Middleton.

How do I know all this? I asked her. I had to. She had been sitting for four days in a lawn chair about 50 yards from an outdoor stage right behind where the kids dance at the Inside Out Soul Festival. Four days of the most current Christian music is played at the festival, which is held at the summer site of a ski resort in the mountains of New Hampshire. I had spotted her from the stage, sitting there smiling, as I opened that Sunday's events with a festival version of "church." I saw her again after four hours of steady punk, hip-hop, and hard rock, still in her lawn chair and still smiling. She was wearing a little red hat. I was too embarrassed to ask her age, but if it wasn't 65, it was 70.

I couldn't resist finding her and talking to her. She was such an unlikely soul at this event, and she was so thoroughly enjoying what I thought would have been outside her understanding and appreciation. I surmised she was probably here with a church group of teenagers, or perhaps she was a grandmother of one of the local performers. But when I asked her why she was here, I got an unexpected answer.

"I love music and my husband loved music. He would have enjoyed this so much."

"How did you even know about this event?"

"I heard about it at the Michael Smith concert."

"Do you like this music?" I said, looking over at the stagehands setting up for a version of hip-hop coming up next. A Van Morrison song was blaring over the speakers. The previous act had one unusually loud screaming song, and Anna was right in the vortex of the huge 20-foot wall of arena speakers. "Michael Smith is pretty tame compared to some of this music."

"Oh, I love all kinds of music as long as it's good."

"I guess this is good, then, or you wouldn't be here."

"Oh, yes, its marvelous."

"Did you know any of these groups before you came?"

"No. I only know about Michael Smith."

But Michael W. Smith wasn't on the bill for the weekend. That wasn't why she was here. I was fishing for explanations. "Did you come with anyone?"

"No. I wish the young people from our youth group at church were here but their parents wouldn't let them come."

"Really? Why?"

"They keep a very tight control. Their children only do things within their own youth group and their families."

I wondered about a system that would declare out-of-bounds for the youth group music that Gramma was enjoying. "Does anyone from your church know you're here?"

"Oh, good heavens, no!" (Rebel Anna)

"Have you been here the whole time?"

"Oh, yes, except I did get out of the rain for a little bit on Friday night."

That meant that in three days Anna of Middleton was into her twentieth hour of live rock 'n' roll. I worried about her ears. I worried about the tip of her nose that was unprotected and already red from the sun. But Anna wasn't worried at all. A couple times when I passed through the crowd during the afternoon, I caught her with tears in her eyes.

Anna was living a fearless faith and having a ball doing it. Anna, the senior citizen, was more daring than her church's youth group. This was a church so bent on keeping kids safe from the world that it would view a Christian rock music festival as a threat. It would judge the music as too worldly and the environment too dangerous. There are lots of non-Christians and very marginal Christians living loose moral lives at these events. No telling what might happen to their kids. These are the same types of Christians who would complain about not finding enough instances of the word "Jesus" in the lyrics of many Christian songs. Funny. Anna didn't seem to have any trouble finding Jesus at all that day.

"Are you having a good time?" I asked Anna of Middleton, and her response would have been suspect had I made it up, but I didn't.

"The best three days of my life."

If the goal of Christian parenting is to raise good, well-behaved, Christian kids, then according to some people's standards, we are probably doing pretty well. If our goal is to raise well-adjusted, worldly-wise Christians who as adults can walk into secular society and celebrate faith as an integral part of all they think about and do, well, let's just say... we have a ways to go. The kids from Anna's church were so far removed that even the Christian version of the world wasn't safe enough for them.

Music You Don't Have to Worry About

"It's about your kids, Marty!" yells Doc Brown over the roar of his DeLorean time machine at the end of the first episode of *Back to the Future*. "We've got to do something about your kids!"

Well, from an ad I heard recently on Christian radio, something has been done. Christian music and Christian radio have done something about the kids by providing a safe place for music free from the blaring assault of unchecked rock and rap on commercial radio. The ad ran something like: "Music you don't have to worry about your kids listening to."

Couple that with another ad that ran on the same station claiming good music makes good people, which makes good citizens, which makes a better America, and you have new moral and social grounds for the existence of a Christian subculture. Words such as *clean, safe,* and *wholesome* come to mind.

As popular culture grows more blatantly decadent, we undoubtedly will see this justification for contemporary Christian institutions and products becoming more and more commonplace—the building of a Christian subculture, not as a message-bearer to the world, but as a safe haven from it. In the last few years we have been experiencing a general exodus of Christians from the world's culture and institutions to a safer alternative Christian culture sporting its own growing market and infrastructure.

I have been speaking regularly in Christian colleges across the country for more than 20 years and have noticed this trend manifested in the attitudes and habits of current students. It was not even five years ago that Christian colleges were struggling for new admissions. Not so now. Children who have been in school during the popular Christian school and homeschool boom of the '80s and '90s are now reaching college age. It stands to reason that parents who have used the Christian school to protect their kids from the world would look to the Christian college as their last bastion. As a result, Christian colleges have never enjoyed such success. Many have to turn away qualified students because of limited space and resources. Every college I've visited in the last few years has a building expansion program in place, already fully funded or close to it. Other institutions, that ten years ago were on their last leg, are now thriving.

Many of the students I meet in these colleges listen to nothing but Christian music. These are the same kids that struggle with some of the required college-level reading, as well as with social and scientific theories they need to learn for a liberal arts degree. Their former schools steered clear of controversial literature and modern theories due to the questionable content, language, and unbiblical philosophies they contain. And yet even Christian colleges realize that a transition to the wider world is imminent and that these cultural realities must be faced—better sooner than later—while the support of a Christian environment can guide the deconstruction and reconstruction of faith that is necessary for personal ownership.

I consistently find the students of these colleges to be far more conservative in their cultural views than their teachers. Faculty members tell me they worry greatly over their students' ability to carry a zealous, but untested faith into the larger, unforgiving culture. Would that there were a Christian world these students could graduate into, but, alas, there is not.

What? Me Worry?

I understand the motivating factor behind a subculture that takes parents' worry away. I worry as much as the next guy about my kids—what they listen to, what they see, and what they do. I worry because I can't do anything about it. If I thought I could, I would. In reality, even a Christian college can't keep the world at bay. Every one of these colleges has its share of cynics and rebels, who, for all we know, might be using all their cynical energy to fight for the faith were they out in a non-Christian environment. Here, though, they fight for the right to listen to secular music or watch R-rated movies—nonissues anywhere else.

Ultimately, there's only one thing that can keep me, and any Christian parent, from worrying about my kids. It's the presence in their lives of the Holy Spirit, not a Christian radio station or a Christian college. Not that there aren't good reasons for both of these. But worry isn't one of them.

There is strong reason to question the validity of creating something so that a Christian doesn't have to worry. Helping us not worry may well be harmful itself because it creates a false sense of safety and discourages a thinking, grappling engagement with culture. Maybe it isn't such a bad thing to worry about the music, if by worrying we mean to be aware of it and not just absorb it—to think about it, evaluate it, learn to understand its deeper messages and the philosophies of life out of which it speaks, and make conscious choices in relationship to it. Who is to say Christian music is necessarily culturally and theologically worry-free, anyway?

The safety element, in the end, may be the most unsafe of all. Children who have been protected from the world will sooner or later be defenseless in it. Those who have been grappling with the world and its ideas and developing a discriminating eye and ear have a better chance of not only making it in the world with their faith whole, but of understanding that world and having something to offer it once they get there. Personally, I worry more about parents *not* worrying. Parents who think that all they have to do is put their kids in a safe Christian environment and their worries are over are the ones who should worry about those kids sooner or later having to face the world and its temptations.

But what about kids who go away to college and lose their faith? some will ask. I've been around this question so much that I know it pops into many minds. We hear about Christian kids going to a secular university or to a "liberal" Christian college—one that does not necessarily support the Christian subculture—and coming back with worldly ideas and habits. We hear about those who have lost their faith.

Personally, I think that anyone who "loses" his or her faith probably never had faith to begin with, and we are all better off knowing that. Better to have someone sink in the deep end of the worldly culture pool than to think he can swim in the shallow water of a Christian subculture yet never have his abilities tested. I believe God would rather save a disciple who tried to walk on water and sank than keep everyone safe in the boat. He can always reach the sinking person more easily than he can reach the cynic.

Let's not forget the prayer of Jesus. He asked not that we be removed from the world, but that we be protected from the world while living in the midst of it. His prayer assumed the world is a dangerous place. He offered no hint of any safe places. Jesus tells us in Revelation 3:16 he would prefer to have us "hot" or "cold" when it comes to faith. Those whose "lukewarm" faith rests on the safety of their Christian environment are most often the ones who have the most to lose. Better off to have a real faith in a dangerous world than a false faith in a safe one. Better off having Jesus protect our kids than to think we can do it with enough money and enough Christian things to isolate them. Those who "lose" their faith in a real world are the ones most likely able to find a real faith—some, perhaps, for the first time. Those who bank too much on their safety are the ones who stand a chance of losing more in the end.

Not Safe for Long

Five members of the band creep onto a dark stage midway through a student talent night that is showcasing a Christian university to prospective students and their parents. Four of the members, all students at the university, are in dark suits. The fifth, the lead singer, steps onstage last. Even without stage lighting, he can be seen faintly in the darkness. He is dressed in white, with giant white moth wings attached to his arms and a powdered white face. A spotlight slowly illuminates him as the music begins, making his eyes look like black holes under snow-dusted hair. He looks like a cross between an angel and an emaciated owl. As the drums build to a strong, driving rhythm that underlies cascading guitars, the winged singer begins to half sing, half chant a throaty stream-of-consciousness lyric laced with social mockery and existential despair. The music is driving and highly emotive, and his voice is as chilling as a vampire's. When the band finishes its song, the largely Christian audience sits stunned, not knowing whether to laugh or applaud. The few claps and random snickers that do echo in the hall make for more of an insult than an affirmation.

A few months later, I witness this same group in a downtown rock club known for vaulting bands into the national spotlight. The audience is riveted. Some are dancing wildly. The applause between songs is enthusiastic. Conversations can be overheard about where this group came from and where it might be playing next. Many are filling out cards to get on the fan list. The contrast between these two settings was huge. What was off-putting in one setting is compelling in another.

It's a new kind of dilemma that now exists in Christian music: Christian bands are finding acceptance in the world with music most Christians don't understand. In a *Los Angeles Times* interview with members of Stavesacre (a similar group), one of them commented: "As far as youth pastors bringing groups of kids to shows, they're looking for a certain vibe and aesthetic, and I don't think we even come close to that. Our music isn't uplifting, and I think a lot of people just want something safe."[1]

Safety, as a watchword for Christian music, is seriously being challenged of late by new Christian bands such as this one that are finding general market avenues for their music and not even bothering with the Christian music industry and the expectations that have grown up around it. The talent-night band I heard, both at the Christian university and at the rock club, was anything but safe, and yet its members are all sincere believers. The band consists of philosophy and literature majors with an eye on their culture and an intense desire to have their music taken seriously as art. Their drummer comes from a missionary family and understands cross-cultural experiences, and that's precisely what we have here and why the same band evoked vastly different reactions. This band is caught in a cross-cultural dilemma. The members are Christians, but they are finding the broader culture to be a more welcome place for what they do than the church. Another Stavesacre band member expressed the same dilemma: "Musically it's about people who appreciate art and good music. The bar crowd is down, and they get it. Ninety percent of the Christian kids don't really care about the music at all, but they book us for some reason."

Those people who book them "for some reason" are most likely youth pastors and Christian concert promoters who want music that will provide both a strong witness for Christian kids and an opportunity to preach the gospel to any non-Christians who might come under the influence of the youth group. They are not as concerned about the artistic aspects of the music as they are about providing a safe, alternative cultural experience for Christian teenagers, and they assume all Christian groups have this same goal. One can see how these two approaches can sometimes be at cross-purposes.

I remember in the late '80s, when Christian music was becoming firmly entrenched as a new, growing industry, I made a similar observation of a Christian band that was playing to the wrong audience. I was at the Christian Music Seminar in the Rockies, a summer music extravaganza in

Estes Park, Colorado, that has become a sort of main event for the Christian music industry. Each day this conference ends with a nightly concert featuring 20-minute sets by new and established Christian artists—a kind of showcase of talent, new and old. On one particular night, mostly middle-of-the-road solo artists singing to recorded tracks were inappropriately teamed up with one live rock band known as The Choir. Though this audience was more polite than the university audience, their reaction to the band was much the same. That was when I first realized I was witnessing a cross-cultural experience.

In both cases, the rock bands were playing to the wrong audiences, and their attempts at being understood were doomed from the start. These same kinds of audiences currently represent a subculture with its own demands, desires, and tastes. The more those desires are fulfilled, the more intolerant the subculture becomes. This is a subculture that has become an entity unto itself. It is accustomed to having the world brought to it on a Christian platter. The bands, with an eye to the world, are not paying any attention to the demands of this subculture. In a sense, the bands should not even be in front of these audiences. The two will only frustrate each other. These subcultural audiences want their entertainment a certain way, and those entertainers who are successful are the ones who learn how to give them what they want. Such subcultural kowtowing is the last thing either of these bands wanted to do.

The audience wants safety; the bands want danger. The audience wants a safe Christian world; the band is trying to take the truth into a dangerous non-Christian world. In the end, which group is best prepared for life? The subculture isn't the world most adults live in. For the most part, it is a temporary escape from the real world, and the escapees return no better prepared than when they left.

"Music you don't have to worry about your kids listening to." I don't think so. I worry more about a subculture and a way of thinking that entertains the thought that such a possibility exists. I worry about a subculture that values an alternative to critical thinking. I worry about a subculture that doesn't value the danger—that doesn't need Jesus praying for its protection because there is nothing to worry about. Those who aren't worried because their kids are safely tucked away in a Christian college, or because they have convinced them to listen only to Christian music and Christian radio, are the ones who have the most to lose when their kids inevitably meet the real world, unprepared.

Life is not safe. It was never meant to be. When we try and make it safe, we go against the purposes of God and we remove ourselves from any influence we might have for good in the world.

"Offended?"

Randy, 31, has been in pastoral ministry for six years. He is currently studying Heidegger, preaching grace, and watching as many movies as he can.

I live in two worlds: as an academic in a secular university and a pastor in the Christian subculture. To do this, I have to lead two different lives. If certain Christians from my church were to follow me around for a day, they would try to get me fired. If they knew I counseled people while we're having a beer, I would lose my job. My lifestyle in one world is an offense in the other. It forces me to live a lie, and I don't want to lie, but I am left no choice. If I lived totally the way the church wants me to live, I would lose my ministry in the world.

The idea—that Christians are always being offended by the world—is damaging to the church. I hate that word, "offended." We should eliminate it from a Christian's vocabulary.

When Christians say they are afraid of being offended by the world, they really mean they are afraid of being tainted. They don't want the evil world to start seeping into their nice, pure Christian lives. So now, they don't watch certain movies or go certain places or have certain people as friends because these associations might taint their holiness. That's not even biblical. Jesus said you don't get sinful by watching something or hearing something bad or hanging out with sinful people; you are already sinful in your heart. If we're not going to be around offensive people, who are we going to witness to, I wonder? I guess we're supposed to look for relatively clean sinners.

What's more, these Christians are not satisfied to sit in their own smug self-righteousness bubble; they have to judge other

Christians, like me, who don't see the world the way they do. Now they're offended by me as well, because I do things they take offense at.

This attitude renders the church powerless in culture. How can you engage with the world when you can't even be around normal people? The only friends these Christians can have are other holy people like themselves.

Then I get the "weaker brother" argument. Church members who are offended when they hear I use a clip from an R-rated movie in my teaching tell me that offends them. These people, who may have been Christians all their lives, still want to qualify as the weaker brother. How long do they plan on staying weak, I wonder?

You know what I really wish I could do? Tie these people to chairs, force them to see *Pulp Fiction* or *American Beauty,* and then say, "OK, let's talk about it now."

—Randy

CHAPTER NINE

It's a Jungle Out There

---— ✐ ——---

The Big Kahuna

The Big Kahuna, starring Kevin Spacey and Danny DeVito, is a movie all Christians should see, especially those who want to have a fearless faith. It's a rare Hollywood movie these days that gives an Evangelical some depth of character, and this one does. It actually portrays a Baptist as looking and thinking somewhat like a Baptist. Some would say that the presence of bad language and sacrilegious comments make this film unsuitable for Christian viewing. I would say these are the very things that make viewing the film mandatory. Besides, Christians in the workplace deal every day with the situations and the language presented in this film.

Based on a play by Roger Rueff called *Hospitality Suite*, the story features three sales representatives of an industrial lubricant company who are attending a business conference in Wichita, Kansas. These salesmen are preparing to host a reception in the hospitality suite of a hotel. The sole purpose of the reception is to meet the president (the Big Kahuna) of a large company and land a huge contract for their own company. As it turns out, Bob, a young Baptist on his first sales trip, is the only one of the three who has a shot at meeting the man. When he does meet him, he ends up witnessing to him about Christ rather than talking business. Bob's Christianity, though not the theme, is an important subtext that mirrors both Bob's zeal and his inexperience in sales and in life.

The irony of the story for Christians is that while Bob is off witnessing to the Big Kahuna, the other two guys are having a "real" conversation about God and the meaning of life. One of them appears very close to becoming a believer. It's a conversation that Bob would have given his right arm to be a part of, but he hasn't yet gained the trust of the other two salesmen, nor is his faith believable to them. Bob's faith, though genuine, is too much about what a Christian should and shouldn't do. This doesn't make him sensitive to his business partners and their spiritual needs. He isn't even sensitive to his own spiritual needs. As one of his partners points out to him, Bob hasn't lived long enough to regret anything. His Christianity, like his experience as a salesman, is, as of yet, untested.

Many of us, like Bob, have more answers than we know what to do with. But our faith needs to be tested by the real questions of both our own lives and the lives of non-Christians around us, and too many of us are not listening to them. As one growing up in the Christian subculture and attending a Christian college, I faced many of the questions the world typically poses, but I faced them in mock review, like a pilot using a flight simulator. As a young man, I was about as prepared as Bob was for talking with unbelievers. I quickly learned that the answers that work in practice don't always work in life. The irony is that many needful Christians will never see this film or be taught by it because of its R-rating.

In an attempt to remain pure and unsullied by the world, Christians are being forced into a tragic compartmentalization of faith and life. Bob exemplifies this segregation in *The Big Kahuna*. He sacrifices his connection with everyday life in order to be pure and unsullied. We get the feeling from the movie that Bob can't wait to get out of that hotel room and back to his new wife and church friends who believe as he does. He is like a fish out of water. He is in a dangerous place. His faith could really grow through an honest encounter with his colleagues, but unfortunately, he is not willing to be vulnerable to such a thing.

Some Christians would rule that Bob was being a powerful Christian for choosing to talk to the Big Kahuna about Christ instead of industrial lubricants. But in fact, his faith was not fearless enough. Bob saw his responsibility to witness as separate from his responsibility as a salesman, when in fact they are one and the same. To talk to the Big Kahuna about industrial lubricants is as spiritual and as important to God as talking to the Big Kahuna about Christ. One talk may lead to the other, but the ultimate salvation of the Big Kahuna does not rest in Bob.

Bob doesn't see it that way. He sees work as a bad place—a necessary evil that forces him to be in the company of people who offend him by their unrighteousness and have little value to him beyond being either potential converts or enemies before whom he must defend his faith. It's also a place where he has to witness, or their blood is on his hands. The Bobs of the world can't leave that blood on the cross with Jesus.

A Sermon No One Can Preach

I am reminded of a story I heard from a Christian journalist who was addressing a roomful of evangelical pastors and seminary students about their need to explain their culture as well as the word of God. His talk was peppered with references to popular songs, TV shows, and current films. After he finished, a Baptist preacher waved him over and asked privately what the journalist thought of the movie *Thelma and Louise*. The movie was having a major impact at the time, and the leading actresses, Susan Sarandon and Geena Davis, had ended up on the cover of *Time* magazine with the headline, "Why *Thelma and Louise* Strikes a Nerve." The journalist had to admit that he hadn't seen the movie, but he had collected a large file of reviews and commentaries on how the movie had sparked the nation's growing controversy over sex roles.

When two other Baptist ministers cornered him with the same question about the same movie, the journalist realized he had unearthed a sticky dilemma. All three pastors had seen the movie and agreed that it was significant. All three knew some women in their congregations who had also seen the movie and were talking about it, raising the question of why these women would relate to a story about wife abuse and anger. Yet when the journalist suggested to the pastors that the subject might be worth a sermon, all three pastors immediately backed down. This was a sermon they could never preach. The subject was too emotionally volatile, they said, and their congregations would be upset that they even referred to an R-rated movie from the pulpit, much less indicated that the questions it raised had anything to do with church. The journalist, Terry Mattingly, in an essay in

The Big Idea of Biblical Preaching, concluded his recollection of these conversations with the haunting question: "So you send your people to the mall and the movie multiplex to find sermons on these kinds of life-wrenching issues?"[1]

The dilemma these pastors were facing is shared by many Christians today: a Christian worldview that is inadequate to handle what most of us are actually doing in the world. On the one hand, there still exists for many Christians remnants of the old notion that they are not supposed to be partaking in culture to any great extent. On the other hand, Christians are partaking of it more than ever. This has created a level of discomfort for some and a sort of spiritual schizophrenia for others—where the right hand doesn't know what the left hand is doing.

If faith is to address what we actually do in the world, then one of two things has to happen: either we get a bigger, more fearless faith—a faith that actually does connect up with all of life—or we have to go back to a more restricted lifestyle where faith and life remain separate, safe, and small. To continue to have a faith that cannot address how we entertain ourselves, how we date and marry, what we do on a Saturday night, how we play a sport, or how we sell industrial lubricants is to have a faith that is largely irrelevant to life. It means our relationship with God feeds only one small area of life instead of nourishing the whole.

We need not think that cultural involvement is met with silence from God. God is interested in everything we do. He is interested in everything that is human, since he made us all in his image. "Most of us spend so much time working, it would be a shame if we couldn't find God there," says Gregory F. A. Pierce, author of *Spirituality@Work.*[2]

A large part of having a fearless faith involves being culturally aware. If we're going to be more culturally aware as Christians (and it appears we are) then we have a responsibility to let God in on it—to see everything through the eyes of faith. To the degree that we do will be the degree to which we can experience God in everything.

This Isn't About You

One popular argument today holds that for our own good, we as Christians should distance ourselves from sinful people. This argument comes always with an underlying conviction that our sensibilities will most certainly be offended by the indecent behavior, the foul language, and the dirty jokes of people who do not have the same Christian conscience we do.

I recently heard a credible rebuttal to this argument. It came from a theology professor who extracted it from an observation he made of his own children. One child was having a birthday party; the other was expressing jealousy over all the attention going to his sibling. Upon discovering this, Dad pulled the selfish child aside and delivered the corrective, "Look this isn't about you. This is about your sister. It's her birthday, not yours."

Suddenly, the professor realized that Jesus would do the same thing. He would pull us aside as we worried that our own sense of holiness might be offended by the unrighteousness of the world around us and gently—or maybe not so gently—correct our spiritual pride and selfishness by focusing our attention in the proper direction. "Look...this isn't about you. This is about your neighbors. It's their turn now. It's their salvation that needs to be important to you, not your own righteousness." To which he could even add,

"...and don't worry so much about your own righteousness. I'm in charge of that, anyway."

As Christians in the world, we are to be focused on people in the world and their need. This is not a time to be focused on ourselves—even on our holiness. Jesus is our example in this. Certainly no one was more holy than he was—the true Son of God who embodied all the fullness of his Father (Colossians 1:19)—and yet we also see him fully enmeshed in a sinful, worldly society. As a friend of sinners, you can believe Jesus got an earful and an eyeful. You don't hang out with sinners without seeing and hearing about their sin. Of course, this will bother you—it must have bothered Jesus—but you simply figure out a way to get over it because this isn't about you. A case could be made that this was, in fact, the attitude of Jesus, who gave up his right to be God and took on the form of a servant because this wasn't about him. It was about us (Philippians 2:5-8).

Remember Lot? He was Abraham's nephew who lived in Sodom, that sinful place from whence we get our word "sodomy." He was the one whose wife was turned into a pillar of salt when she looked back at the burning city as the rest of her family escaped God's wrath upon Sodom. Poor Lot. We rarely give the guy a fair shake—probably because he went into a deep depression after losing his home and his wife and drank himself into doing some pretty stupid things. And yet, in the New Testament we find out that "...living among them day after day, [Lot] was tormented in his righteous soul by the lawless deeds he saw and heard" (2 Peter 2:8).

Lot had a righteous soul? You'd never guess that from reading the Old Testament account. You would think he would have been pretty happy about escaping Sodom and having God torch the place. Instead, he wanted God to spare the city. Yes, Lot was bothered by the evil around him, but this wasn't about him. This was about a city full of sinners, some of whom were his friends. If it seems hard to imagine some of the people of Sodom being Lot's friends, we need look no further than the friends of Jesus. This is not about becoming insensitive to sin; it's about overcoming what bothers us about sin because we care about sinners.

If Lot's righteous soul was tormented day after day, you can imagine the torment Jesus must have gone through continually, and yet we never hear of it. We only hear of his compassion for the lost and his quickness to forgive. Somehow, he found a way to get over the offense. Perhaps it was the knowledge that he would soon pay the price for every sin that he witnessed. Perhaps it was his ability to see past the offense and into the heart. In any case, if Jesus could get over the offensiveness of sinners for the sake of their eternal souls, then I'm sure he can help us do the same.

Seeing someone else's sin should only be a reminder of our own sin and the glorious forgiveness we have received from Christ. Being bothered by the unrighteousness of those around us is most likely an indication that we have not sufficiently faced our own unrighteousness. The way I see it, there are only two ways to look at this. We can condemn the world and hope God gets us out of here before it burns, or we can take the more dangerous route and stick it out here and learn to love sinners—seeing in them our own forgivability and loving them unconditionally, the way we are loved by God through Christ.

It's for The Kids

When my daughter graduated from high school, she wanted to celebrate her last few weeks of school by hosting a party at which her older brother's punk band would play. Since our backyard had little room for a stage, much less an audience, we started to investigate the idea of having our event in the middle of our street.

Now to understand the significance of this, one must grasp the new face of suburban America. Gone are the front porches, front lawns, sidewalks, and driveways that once defined American neighborhoods. Children have little room to play; older kids have little room to hang out. There is no Main Street that defines downtown now, only a wide, divided avenue that alternates between planned community and convenience mall.

Our particular street was a pseudo-cul-de-sac with nine two-story houses facing each other. I call it "pseudo" because in most culs-de-sacs, you can turn your car around while maintaining forward motion. Our street simply stopped— a street so narrow, you could not turn around without backing up. The houses were no more than ten feet apart and fifty feet across from each other, with bedrooms and shallow balconies perched over two-car garages at the end of driveways that were all of five feet long.

"It's perfect," said my son, the drummer of the band, as he surveyed the potential concert scene. "We can put the stage at the end of the street and the sound will bounce off all these garage doors. We can even shoot videos from the balconies." He was right. We lived in a virtually untested outdoor Street-O-Rama concert hall.

The real test, however, was mine. How do you get a community living this close together yet so far apart in genuine relationships to support something like this? How do you have an outdoor event for teenagers without the event's either getting crashed by wandering hordes of suburban gangs looking for action or shut down by an irate neighbor whose peace will undoubtedly be disturbed? And then there was the issue of potential lawsuits. What if someone gets hurt, or a cigarette causes a fire, or kids come drunk and start a fight, or someone gets injured in a mosh pit and sues the band, sues me, sues my neighbors, sues the manufacturer of the street, sues the homeowners association, and sues anyone else who happens to be walking by at the time. The deputy sheriff thought I was crazy to do this and expected to be getting a call from me later that night. Some neighbors thought I was insane. The captain of the firehouse thought I was courageous. Even the friends I called for help had other things to do. And my wife, whose ideas and energy sparked this event in the first place but who was out of town on business when all the setup needed to be done, said she was sorry for getting me into this.

None of us could foresee what began as a friendly party with a $500 sound system mushrooming into a $2,500 CD release showcase, including staging, lights, security guards, special-event insurance, two-way radios, T-shirts, tables, bottled water, and a Porta-Potty.

No wonder all the concert promoters I know seem to have attention deficit disorder. They must thrive on danger-induced adrenaline. They must get a rush out of being one step away from bankruptcy or jail. They must have to be experiencing sheer terror in order to get blood to their brains. I, on the other hand, lived for the last three weeks on the edge of panic, working my way through each new, unnerving challenge with a vow that I would never do this again.

To try to head off opposition at the pass, we printed up fliers and distributed them to every house in our neighborhood. We announced when the concert would be, and we invited everyone to come. It turned out to be a good thing because quite a few kids showed up—some of them racing their cars around our tiny streets. Believe me, this was not your nice local church group event. My kids didn't know half the kids that showed up.

I was running up the stairs at the front gate, where I had been parking director for an hour, when my son started the festivities with a five-minute drum solo. I couldn't see him, but I could hear the sounds from his drums rumbling off garage doors down the streets of my neighborhood. These were the same drums that had been shut up inside our house for so many years of practicing. I rounded the corner as the high-energy music started up and found a crowd of 250 kids pressing the stage, moshing in the street in front of our house. A number of my neighbors had shown up, some of whom I met for the first time.

As it turned out, there were no irate phone calls, the police didn't have to show up, no one got hurt, and some of my kids' friends stayed and cleaned up the street afterward. We actually did receive three calls the next day. They were compliments from neighbors who were glad that we were doing something nice for the kids.

We didn't change the world that day, we didn't save any souls, we didn't usher in the millennium, but we gave my daughter a fitting celebration and my son a place to play drums. We gave a bunch of kids a good time and brought out a few neighbors. For a year that also included the tragedy of Columbine, this was significant.

It's a dangerous world. There are huge risks in getting involved. We can do as most people do: shut our garage door behind us and retreat into our safe haven of a home. We can come out only to go to work, to church, or to social events planned by the church or other Christians. That would be the safe thing to do.

Or we can do the dangerous thing and get out on the street and meet our neighbors—maybe even organize a block party. Sure, we'll be at risk, but look at where serving our safety has gotten us. We're all hiding—our neighbors included. Wouldn't it be great if Christians started coming out?

"Their Only Glimpse of Christ Is Me"

Cris is 23 and married. She works as a career advocate for an independent living center. She grew up in a Christian family and was the first in her family to attend college. While still in college, she witnessed numerous children with disabilities being labeled, made fun of, and ignored by the very staff and teachers who were supposed to be helping these children. She now works in one of those staff positions, seeking to change that picture.

I deal on a daily basis with bridging the non-Christian/Christian gap. I work for an organization that promotes inclusion of all people with disabilities. I love my job and I believe in what I do. I also love Christ with all my heart. This is no secret at my workplace.

Recently, I have been gaining respect from non-Christians who have been put off by in-your-face Christianity. How can we expect people to live by the rules of Christianity when they don't know the reasons behind the rules? I don't feel I have had to compromise my beliefs to reach my co-workers; I just try to make all my efforts love based. But I have come across Christians who are very upset about my approach.

Most Christians I meet don't necessarily have a problem with my job itself. (I say most because recently I became acquainted with a group of Christians who believe all children with disabilities, especially cognitive disabilities, are the result of direct generational curses from God.) Problems *do* arise when some Christians find out I work with people who don't believe in Christ, are homosexual or support it, support abortion, voted for Gore, swear, drink, or do any combination of these things.

My witnessing is often scrutinized when I question more direct evangelism methods.

I rub elbows every day with people whose only glimpse of Christ is me. They are used to the hate crimes, picket signs, and angry words that sometimes accompany Christian witness. They tell me they don't listen to all that, and I don't blame them. They know how I feel, and they respect me. I think they see a different side of Christianity in me—one that intrigues them. Over lunch, my boss has actually asked me to share my faith with her. This is the same woman whom I have heard numerous times complain about Christians and how they treat people.

I love seeing God work at my workplace—the last place some of my fellow Christians would expect to find him. I pray for God to work through me and protect me every day. None of this is possible without him.

—Cris

CHAPTER TEN

Coming Out

―――――――❧―――――――

A Dangerous Night?

Here's something to think about: Is Halloween a holiday that should be avoided at all costs—or does it provide a perfect opportunity for a neighborhood "coming out" of sorts? For it to be the latter will take rethinking on the part of some believers. Fearing the worst on an evening many Christians believe celebrates the wiles of the devil, some choose to have no part in the traditional neighborhood trick-or-treating that accompanies October 31, formerly known as All Hallows Eve (All Saints' Eve).

This boycott of neighborhood dressing up and doorbell ringing is relatively new on the Christian scene, at least in my experience. As a child in an evangelical Christian home, I was right in there with all the other gremlins and witches on our block trying to scare as many Snickers bars as I could out of our neighbors' stashes and into my bulging pillowcase. And you can be sure that every home on my block was always duly prepared to be scared by us.

The anti-Halloween movement among Christians didn't catch my attention until after my own kids had outgrown this annual neighborhood siege. So you can imagine the shock and surprise on the face of the pastor's wife who came up to me after I gave a talk on Christian worldview and wanted to know what I did with my children on Halloween. When I told her I helped them into their costumes, put on a monkey mask, turned up "Ghostbusters" on the stereo, and hit the streets with the express purpose of scaring all the neighborhood ghosts and goblins before they scared me, her face turned white. Apparently what was OK for my parents in 1958 and my wife and me in 1988 was no longer acceptable Christian behavior for a new millennium.

The more acceptable Christian thing to do now on Halloween is to close up the house and have an alternative party for our kids at church. The party usually has a harvest or biblical character theme—no ghosts or goblins allowed. Though I understand how this safer alternative came to be, I wonder whether a blanket boycott is the only way to handle this controversial holiday. Is this just one more time when we as Christians isolate ourselves from the rest of our culture for religious reasons apparent only to us? Have we really thought through what our dark houses are saying to the rest of the block while we're off having our alternative party? I can hear the neighborhood kids shuffling by our house, saying, "Don't go there, they don't give anything." Is this what we want to be known for in the community—a dark house on the one night you can be guaranteed neighbors will visit?

My kids are older now, but when they were little, Halloween in the Massachusetts town they grew up in was nothing short of an informal neighborhood progressive party. I'd start out with my immediate neighbor and his kids and then run into other parents standing outside other houses. Soon we were a small crowd making our way up and down the street while tired little feet slogged through the fallen leaves of October. By the time the kids had filled their bags, I had been in and out of a number of homes, met people I never knew, started some relationships, and renewed others. Meanwhile, my wife was home dumping huge handfuls of candy into open bags, raving over costumes, inviting kids to come back and visit whenever they wanted, and entertaining other parents that I missed. It was a major community event and opened many doors for fruitful relationships we were able to continue the rest of the year.

I don't want to diminish the reality of spiritual warfare—something to be taken seriously by all believers—but the last day of October is not a spiritual battle any more than any other day. If Satan comes out on Halloween, he doesn't go back into hiding the next morning. Regardless of the origins of Halloween (and there appears to be little agreement about this, even among historians), what we have today is a culturewide event that is more concerned with pretending than it is with the underworld. It's actually one holiday that adults haven't taken over—the one time kids get to "be" whatever they want to be. Our participation—or lack thereof—in such a popular, cultural event is more indicative of our interaction with the world around us than it is a measure of our stance in a fight between good and evil. If Satan wins anything on this day, he may win more through the darkened homes of Christians than through anything else.

The truth is, Christians never have anything to fear—on this night or any other—or else God is not God and his promises are not true. What we ought to be concerned about instead is a retreat from our homes, when, more than any other time, it's important to be there with our lights on and a bowl full of treats near the door.

"I'm Staying"

Contemplating how we as Christians deal with Halloween yields more than practical advice about the biblical injunction to be a neighbor. It is also a good metaphor for a fearless faith. What do we do when it gets dangerous for us in the world? Darken our houses and go to the church or stay home and leave our lights on? Or to put it another way: Do we retreat to the safety of a Christian subculture or do we stay put in a dangerous world—even go out into it, in costume, and mingle with the neighbors?

Georgian Banov was once a rock star in Bulgaria. He came to America in the early '70s seeking fame and fortune and found Christ instead. Like other talented musicians in those early days of contemporary Christian music, Georgian translated his newfound faith into a musical career and formed a group. He called it Silverwind. It enjoyed considerable success.

By the late '80s, Georgian's soul grew restless for his home, and his heart began to hurt for the spiritual needs of his country. Realizing that political changes had given him new access to his roots, he prepared to return to Bulgaria via some new opportunities, cashing in on his still-popular status in that country as a rock singer.

One of those opportunities involved recording a new album in London. This would not be a Christian album (Europe doesn't have a Christian market separate from the mainstream as we do in America), but he wanted a product that would be popular and still reflect his faith. As if to prepare him for his reentry into the world without the support and security of a Christian subculture, God gave him an experience he would never forget. Georgian told me about his experience, and I haven't forgotten it either. It always reminds me of the vision God gave Peter to help Peter get over his bias toward the Jews and realize the gospel was going to go further than just his people (Acts 10:9-35).

Georgian was considering signing with a respected producer in London when the man invited him to a local hot spot to hear a popular new band he had just finished recording. The place turned out to be a punk music club where Georgian found himself jammed into a mass of androgynous humanity that was jumping, screaming, and sweating as the group on stage pumped frenzied energy into the room. Georgian, somewhat sick to his stomach, had decided he'd seen enough of this pagan display and started for the door; but as he tried to force his way through the undulating crowd, he heard another voice over the din of the decibels that were shaking the walls. Much to his surprise, he distinguished the voice as the voice of God in his inner ear. Georgian knew it was God because God had spoken to him before in the same way. And he knew it was God because the voice was telling him something so far from his own mind and spiritual sensitivities that it was revolutionary. He would not have thought of this himself. The message was similar to the one God gave Peter when he told Peter to rise and eat that which had formerly been religiously unclean to him. The voice in Georgian's head said, "Go ahead and leave if you want to, but I'm staying."

Did Jesus come into our world only to touch down for a brief lifetime and endure our awfulness until he couldn't handle it any more? I hope not, because that means he escaped back to heaven and left us alone—that he couldn't stand our presence. How can we possibly say God can't tolerate the world when he can put up with Christians—even take up residence within us through his Holy Spirit? Jesus left, but he also left his Spirit, and his Spirit had better stay, or there is no hope for any of us.

The truth is, the world makes us uncomfortable. The world makes us sick to our stomachs sometimes. The world makes us want to leave. The question we must ask, however, is: Are we abandoning the world to darkness to make ourselves more comfortable in the light?

Would I have been with Jesus in the middle of tax collectors and sinners at Matthew's house, or would I have been off to the side with the Pharisees wondering what Jesus was doing there? If I had been in the middle with Jesus, it surely would have been uncomfortable, with the crowd of tax collectors and sinners all around me holding their goblets a little unsteadily and asking me, much too close to my face, who I was, and what I was all about, and who was this guy Jesus, and was I with him, and what was this new thing Levi was getting into, and why, for God's sake, was Levi leaving tax collecting just when the economy was on the upswing, thanks to Caesar?

Jesus was there because Matthew invited him. And Jesus didn't seem to mind. Nowhere do you get the impression that Jesus was out of place at this party, or uncomfortable. On the contrary, it appears he was quite happy about it, for when he was questioned by the Pharisees as to why he associated with these social misfits, he replied, "It is not the healthy who need a doctor, but the sick. I have not come to call the righteous, but sinners to repentance" (Luke 5:31-32). Put that another way: I didn't come this far to hang out with good people. I came for the bad guys.

In effect, Jesus stood in the middle of Matthew's house with sinners all around him and told the Pharisees, "Go ahead and leave if you want to, but I'm staying." He still stands today in the middle of the world that he loves and came to die for. He calls us to do the same.

"I've Already Left"

But I wonder if I'm getting ahead of myself. God's message to Georgian came at a time in Georgian's life when he was already moving out from his comfortable Christian environment into the world. No more nice Christian record company people excited about his ministry. He had moved on to standard business people who wanted to know if he could hack it in the music world. No more safe Christian audiences in America. He was on his way back to a potentially hostile audience in an Eastern bloc country. He was on his way out of the comfort zone. His issue at that time was contemplating going back. He got himself out there and then had second thoughts.

But some Christians haven't had the *first* thought. Some are too firmly entrenched in the subculture to even try to get out. For these people, God might have a different take on this. He might just be saying: "You can stay there where it's safe if you want to, but I've already left."

Not Without a Witness

Truth is: God is already out in the world—he always has been—and he is not waiting for us before he takes action. I always find it exciting, provocative, and somewhat amusing when God shows up in the world without the aid of Christians and our overrated Christian subculture.

In the mid-1990s, an obscure piece of music that defied categorization surfaced in the British pop world and sparked interest among certain circles in America. It's a recording that ignores all the rules of pop music. It takes considerable time and patience to absorb it, and for that reason its relative success took everyone by surprise. The recording is more likely to be found in the classical section of a record store as opposed to pop or rock, but people manage to find it anyway.

The entire piece lasts more than an hour and fifteen minutes and consists of a tape loop of an old British bum continuously singing the same gospel chorus. His thin, meager voice is gradually accompanied by a full orchestra, chorus, and, finally, the deep, resonate, gravelly voice of Tom Waits.

According to its creator, Gavin Bryars, the idea for this unusual recording came when he first inherited leftover tape from a documentary about homeless people living in and around London. The old British bum and his song had been captured by accident. Intrigued by the emotional power of this one simple chorus and the vulnerable quality of the transient's voice, Bryars made a tape loop of the four-line lyric and began experimenting with chordal accompaniment using his old upright piano at home. The piano was out of tune just enough to be in tune with the old man's voice.

The result is a highly unusual and fascinating piece of music that builds ever so slightly upon each pass of the man's little song. Starting with just the bare voice itself, complete with ambient street sounds, the recording of the old man's voice is joined first by a string quartet, then gradually a full orchestra, first featuring low strings, then the higher strings, then a choir that almost drowns out the man's voice. Finally Tom Waits sings a duet with him, working his voice in and around the voice of the homeless man, rejuvenating it and bringing it new life. Listening to this CD is like watching a clock: You can't really see the hands move, you are just suddenly aware that they are in a position different from the one they were in a few minutes earlier.

Once, while leaving the tape loop of the man's unaccompanied voice repeating in the studio, Bryars returned from getting a cup of coffee to find the normally lively room, in his words, "unnaturally subdued. People were moving about much more slowly than usual, and a few were sitting quietly weeping."[1] That's when he knew he had something powerful and profound.

The lyrics to the simple song are childlike and straightforward gospel.

> *Jesus' blood never failed me yet, never failed me yet*
> *Jesus' blood never failed me yet*
> *This one thing I know*
> *For he loves me so.*[2]

And around and around it goes for an hour and fifteen minutes.

Seventy-five minutes of this relentless testimony begins to have an unmistakable effect on the listener. You slowly realize that this man possesses something in his poverty that transcends what so many seek in wealth. It is the kind of irony that forced Gavin Bryars to say in his liner notes, "Though I do not share the simple optimism of his faith, I am still touched by the humanness of his voice. Although the old man died before he could hear what I had done with his singing, the piece remains as a restrained testament to his spirit and optimism."

Where did this come from? There appear to be no Christians involved in this project anywhere except the most important place of all: the old singer himself. Take the accidental capturing of the faith-filled song of a toothless bum, put it with an orchestral arrangement by an avant-garde classical composer who isn't even a believer, and you have not only an unself-conscious, paradoxical proclamation of the hope of the gospel through the secular mouthpiece of pop classical music, you have God doing some really fun stuff out in the world. He's not waiting for anybody. He will not be without a witness.

That Black Streak

His face is gnarled like the bark on an old tree and scarred by the demons of chemical dependency. His voice is deep and rough, as always, and true to its form as a standard in country music for more than four decades. He is the Man in Black—the voice of the down-and-out. He is Johnny Cash, and the faith that has accompanied him for a number of years is coming to the forefront in the later chapters of his life.[3] The man who made himself famous for walking the line is stepping over it these days with unabashed courage.

In another case of God getting his message out without the help of a Christian network affiliate, the simple gospel through Johnny Cash has been showing up consistently in his shows and interviews, some in the most unlikely places, like this interview in *Rolling Stone* magazine.

"You know my album cover with the two dogs on it?" he asked a reporter who was reviewing his 1994 release "American Recordings." "I've given them names. Their names are Sin and Redemption. Sin is the black one with the white stripes; Redemption is the white one with the black stripe. That's kind of the theme of that album, and I think it says it for me, too. When I was really bad, I was not all bad. When I was trying to be good, I could never be all good. There would be that black streak going through."[4]

Not many people could get away with talking about sin and redemption in *Rolling Stone* magazine, unless it was Johnny Cash talking about his dogs. A well-known Christian artist wouldn't have been able to do this without being ridiculed. That's the creative resourcefulness of the Holy Spirit. Just when old guys such as Tony Bennett, BB King, and Cash are getting respect from the younger generation as being the original versions of the music the younger generation now writes and plays, Johnny's faith becomes more important to him than anything. (His pastor often travels with him, and Johnny announces him and makes him available for counseling after his concerts.) The placement and the timing clearly indicate God is behind this. God does not need a subculture to buy time on network television or manipulate the media. He can do just fine with what he has.

"Being Out"

Erik, 34, is a business development executive for a software company. He's married and has three sons.

The tension of following Christ versus following Christianity is a central theme in how I engage in faith. Being "out" of the Christian subculture ironically affords greater freedom in viewing life from a Christian vantage point.

People disarm when you engage on the level of a person (Jesus) instead of an institution (Christianity). It was an epiphany to realize that my reluctance to share my faith was really discomfort with being associated with a conservative, reactionary movement of people who use Christianity as a badge. People who follow movements are unfortunately often the very same ones who retreat from the difficulty of understanding and engaging with those who have a worldview different from their own. I relish the opportunity to have such encounters.

Talking about the person of Jesus is a far more engaging starting point than talking about the four spiritual laws. Being "out" frees our engagement with mainstream culture. The Christian community paints itself into a corner by so narrowly defining what is culturally acceptable. We are our own worst enemy in perpetuating the stereotype of being repressed and simpleminded. I have a close friend who is a pastor, and he laments the incubated life of relating only with Christians. He misses being out. I love being out. Jesus was out. It was the Pharisees who were in the closet.

—Erik

CHAPTER ELEVEN

Gaining Credibility

---------◆◇◆---------

"Work With Me, Children;
Work With Me."

It's too bad that God doesn't have more cooperation from Christians out in the world. Often we don't take advantage of our opportunities—opportunities he may even be creating for us—because we are too busy fighting the world to recognize what God might be doing in it.

For instance, the world seems to be fascinated with the story of the life of Christ. Since the early days of the Jesus movement we have seen musicals such as *Godspell* and *Jesus Christ Superstar*, movies such as *The Greatest Story Ever Told* and *Last Temptation of Christ*, and numerous made-for-television renderings of Christ's life, including a recent creative interpretation of the story of Jesus via animated clay figures.

Now, one would think that these worldly attempts at telling our story would have been met with enthusiasm in the Christian community. What an opportunity! Christians are called to tell the story of Jesus, the Christ, to the world, and here the world is trying to tell the story to itself. But instead of being excited that attempts are made and the subject comes up, in each of the cases mentioned, we sabotage our chances by over-reacting to the world's inability to get the story right. Usually we are offended, reacting as defensive, hurt children rather than mature adults who shouldn't be expecting the world to get it right in the first place. Why should they? They don't believe it, or at the most are struggling with belief.

Still, the idea of Jesus has been brought to the public consciousness. Why not take advantage of that instead of taking it as some sort of personal affront to our beliefs? I don't see God rushing to his own defense. If God isn't defending himself, I don't think he's standing by helplessly hoping we will do it for him. No, it's probably because he has other concerns.

Indeed he does. Over and over in the New Testament, Jesus and Paul and Peter make it clear that these days we are in are not the days of judgment, but the days of salvation. It is a time when God is favorably disposed to the sons and the daughters of mankind. He has postponed his judgment to give all people a chance to respond to his merciful gift of Christ on the cross. God did not postpone judgment so that we could be judgmental in his place. We have his message. We are announcers of the good news or, as Paul calls us, ambassadors of reconciliation (2 Corinthians 5:18-20).

Nor are we God's last line of defense. God can defend himself quite well without us. We don't have to be defensive or offended by these attempts of the world at telling the story, even when they don't get it right. The important thing is: The subject came up and the world brought it up. We can use that to our advantage. Christian journalists can write about it, Christian radio can discuss the question intelligently and culturally, and all of us can use it in our conversations with non-Christians, since the media brought it up in the first place. Talking about Christ would normally be thought of as too religious or culturally irrelevant, and yet here, the world's entertainment culture is dealing with the subject. They opened the discussion; we didn't. "Did you hear about the movie/play/musical? Just who was Jesus anyway? Who do you think he was?" What a great place to begin.

Breaking the Stereotype

In a recently published interview with screenwriter and television producer Coleman Luck, Mary Cagney of *Christianity Today* explored the cultural clashes between Evangelicals and Hollywood that have come as the result of defensive Christianity. As a Christian and an executive with Universal Studios, Mr. Luck is in a unique position to see both sides of an ideological fence. For instance, Evangelicals cannot believe Hollywood is motivated by anything other than money, and Hollywood can't avoid stereotyping faith in either the phony garb of liberal Catholicism or the religious window dressing of right-wing politics.

Luck recalls how during all the brouhaha over the movie *Last Temptation of Christ*, some powerful, wealthy Christians made an attempt to purchase the negatives of the movie in order to take the movie off the market. The message that spread around Hollywood had these Christians in effect saying, "You people are just whores, and the only thing you care about is money—so here's the money."[1] There was little attempt on the part of the Christian public to at least consider the possibility that this movie may have been a serious effort on someone's part to find something real about the life of Christ, however biblically uninformed it might have been.

On the other side of the fence, Hollywood is constantly portraying people of faith as ugly and cheap. Christians and religious fanatics are always gumming up the works. Faith is rarely pictured in movies or on television as something intelligent, evenhanded, or normal. Robert Duvall's character, Sonny, in the Oscar-nominated film *The Apostle*, possesses a faith uncharacteristically believable by Hollywood standards. Yet he is still portrayed as a guy who doesn't seem to be playing with a full deck, and certainly not someone many Christians would want to model their lives after. If Hollywood were to even hint at similar negative stereotyping in relation to gender, sexual orientation, or race, they would be soundly chastised by both the media and the public.

Life has got to be quite interesting for Coleman Luck, who must straddle these misconceptions every day. The most memorable account of this tension was a story he told about the protests that went on outside Universal's television studios over *Last Temptation of Christ*.

"I remember driving with a friend through a crowd of people who were shoving placards in front of our car with 'John 3:16' written on them. They were Christians, but believe me, they didn't look very loving. My friend, who was not a Christian and was a producer for *The Equalizer*, turned to me and said, 'I would hate these people if I didn't know you.'"[2]

In that one simple reaction is captured the most powerful weapon available to combat the assumptions, ideologies, stereotypes, and misconceptions that accompany

Christianity today: a Christian in a mutually respectful relationship with a non-Christian. It's our life, our friendship, and our integrity that will make a difference in the world, and that difference can best be known through personal relationship. If I might put words in the other man's mouth, I would guess, by his statement, that he was saying: *The fact that you are a Christian and I find you to be a credible person makes me think twice about these people who do not seem credible to me. You make me think. You challenge the assumption. You break the stereotype. If I didn't know you, I would hate these people, but since I do know you, I have to give these people, and your faith, another chance.*

In the Car or in the Crowd?

Picture again Coleman Luck, a Christian, on his way to work, but he can't get to work because of a crowd of Christians protesting his place of work. This poignant encounter illustrates two very different approaches by which Christians can make a mark on society. One is how we have been going at this for some time, the other is how we need to be doing it now. One is safe, the other is fearless. One makes enemies, the other is effective in bringing people to Christ.

Put yourself in the crowd and you can see why the protest approach is so appealing. Being part of the crowd gives a sense of power. After all, 3,000 people marching on Universal Studios can't be wrong. The crowd earns attention. This protest will no doubt be covered by the media. You'll be able to watch yourself on the six o'clock news. In the crowd there is safety in numbers. Those around you insulate you from any hostile forces. As part of the crowd, you don't have to speak for yourself because the group has a spokesperson to speak for you. Most of all, in the crowd, you feel like you are really doing something about how bad the world is. You might actually shut down a studio for a day. That's better than sitting home feeling as if the world is getting worse and worse and you can't do anything about it.

Now contrast that by putting yourself in the car. In the car you feel weak and vulnerable, but that means you have to find your strength in the Lord. In the car, you feel like no one notices you. You simply plug away day after day at your job, seeking to follow God and do what's right. The guy next to you knows you are a Christian, but he sees you as different from all the Christians he doesn't like. This makes you feel good, but you often wonder how much of an impact you are actually having.

Going to work each day, in the car, is like going into a danger zone. You are constantly encountering non-Christians and non-Christian values, and holding onto a faith, with integrity, is very hard. As if this weren't enough, you have to fight the friendly fire of fellow Christians who are in the crowd working against the credible, loving Christian life you are trying to exemplify.

You are often tempted to compromise your faith, and you have to think about what hill you are willing to die on. You believe that as a producer (or whatever it is that you do), you may be able to effect some small change on society, but most of the time you feel pretty insignificant. When it comes to issues of faith, you must speak for yourself. You have no one to speak for you. This means you must work hard at articulating your faith in terms that non-Christians will be able to understand. In short, your life outside the comfort of a Christian environment is dangerous and challenging, but if pressed, you would agree that even if you sometimes complain, you would not have it any other way.

It was through a working friendship with Coleman Luck that an unbeliever was prevented from discounting Christianity. The unbeliever's damaging stereotype of Christians was broken by real lives in relationship. The benefits of a fearless life of faith have to be encountered in and through a human relationship with someone who knows God and yet has not lost touch with the world. It will be known through such straddlers of culture as Coleman Luck, for that is what we all must be—citizens of heaven and citizens of earth at the same time. Christians with a fearless faith will find themselves in a position to break prejudicial stereotypes. In evangelism, it's often not what you know, but who you know. If our witnessing attempts fail, it is likely because these attempts are based only on telling people what we know, and not on getting to know them as well.

Good At Something

For the sake of the illustration, let's think of the car in which Coleman Luck was carpooling with his producer friend that morning as a potential place of influence in which you are establishing a personal relationship of mutual respect, even with those outside the Christian subculture. Consider, then, how Coleman Luck got in the car in the first place. He earned the right to be there by being a good producer. That's pretty much true for any endeavor. You get in the car by being good at something.

It's important to note here that being in the car includes having a Christian influence. Coleman Luck's friend knew Coleman was a Christian. You may get in the car and remain quiet about your faith to begin with, but your faith won't be kept quiet for long. As you gain respect, your faith will gain respect as well. The non-Christian producer does not see Coleman Luck's faith as a barrier to their relationship. It is his credible faith, in fact, that set up the contrast between Coleman and the crowd, calling forth the other producer's statement. If the other producer saw his Christian friend as being like one of the people in the crowd, he never would have been in the car with Coleman. He can respect Coleman's faith even though he does not share it, and, conversely, Coleman can give his friend the right not to believe without forcing him out of the relationship. We are called to be witnesses, not salesmen. My guess is that Coleman Luck has shared his faith with his fellow producer as a natural course of events in his life. But he's not trying to "close a deal" on the man.

C. S. Lewis, in the following quote from *God in the Dock*, tells why a Christian in the car is much more dangerous than a Christian in the crowd.

> I believe that any Christian who is qualified to write a good popular book on any science may do much more by that than any directly apologetic work. The difficulty we are up against is this. We can make people (often) attend to the Christian point of view for half an hour or so; but the moment they have gone away from our lecture or laid down our article they are plunged back into a world where the opposite position is taken for granted.
>
> What we want is not more books about Christianity but more books by Christians on other subjects—with their Christianity latent.
>
> You can see this most easily if you look at it the other way around. Our faith is not very likely to be shaken

by any book on Hinduism. But if whenever we read an elementary book on Geology, Botany, Politics or Astronomy, we found that its implications were Hindu, that would shake us. It is not the books written in direct defense of Materialism that make the modern man a materialist; it is the materialistic assumptions in all the other books. In the same way, it is not books on Christianity that will really trouble (a person). But a person would be troubled if, whenever he wanted a quick introduction to some science, the best work on the market was always by a Christian.[3]

Coleman Luck has, in a sense, written his own book on producing. He's good at it. He's respected for it. He has a number of successful shows under his belt, or he wouldn't have his job. People come to him to find out how to produce, and they encounter, like it or not, a Christian man with a Christian worldview. There could conceivably be some people in the studio who do not like the fact that Coleman Luck is a Christian, but they can't really do anything about that because Mr. Luck is so good at what he does.

If we follow Lewis's argument, then, there are sacred grounds for being secularly smart. Being good at something besides being a Christian is a way in which we gain respect in the world and an opportunity for our faith.

"But...Can You Paint?"

At a PTA meeting once, I sat next to a Jewish woman who had a specific question to ask me when something I said revealed that I was one of those "born again Christians."

"Perhaps you can explain what happened to me just the other day," she said. I said I would try. "Well, this young man stopped by my house to see if I would hire him to paint it. I don't like solicitors so I almost closed the door on him, except that he seemed like such a nice boy and my house did need painting. So I asked him if he had a card he could leave me. When he gave me his card, I noticed it had a fish on it. I asked him what that was for, and he produced a really big smile and said, 'Oh, I'm a Christian painter!' Now what do you suppose he meant by that?"

This was not easy. How do you explain an eager, self-proclaimed Christian house painter to a Jewish mother at a PTA meeting? I tried apologizing for the man's zeal, which had failed to take into account anything other than his own beliefs. The woman assured me she was just fine with that.

"So what did you tell him?" I was curious.

"I told him, 'That's nice…I suppose…but can you paint?'"

It was the operative question. It was the right question. She merely wanted to confirm the obvious. He had clouded the issue by labeling his vocation in religious terms. Some Christians use the sign of the fish as a sort of secret code between Christians that might garner them more business in the Christian community. But outside that community, it only confuses the issue. All the woman did was put things back into terms she could understand. It's as if she said, "I'm not sure about this Christianity of yours, or how it relates to you being a painter, but if you can do a good job painting my house, then I might be interested in hiring you."

We need to realize that this is the main question the world really wants us to answer. Can you paint? Can you produce? Can you write? Can you park cars? Can you teach? Can you do surgery? Can you win a case? Can you take care of my children? Can I trust you? Can you invest my money well? In their minds, our Christianity is our own business, and they are right. Our Christianity is our own business, and it is our story, and we will tell it sometimes when our relationships warrant it.

Maybe after the house is beautifully painted at the right price, and after neighbors have been commenting on the great paint job and inquiring as to the painter, and after numerous conversations have ensued, and after the young man knows something of the woman's life and her Jewish faith because he had the courtesy to ask and took the time to listen…then, when he talks about his faith in Christ (and he will because it's so important to him), it will mean something, like Coleman Luck's faith meant something to the non-Christian producer in the car. And that's much more than will be accomplished by a smiling Christian painter at her door with a fish on his card, or a placard-waving fanatic in the crowd. It's the meaningful testimony of a Christian who loves to paint houses, loves God and his neighbor, and takes pride in his work.

According to C. S. Lewis, the Christian painter at the front door is, in terms of the impact of his faith out in the world, pretty harmless. But the hardworking painter with a respectable job under his belt, an honorable faith in his heart, and a caring relationship with those around him? *That*…is a dangerous man.

"Salt and Light"

Mark grew up in a pastor's home. He has worked as a host for radio and television talk shows, as a fashion model and a model for television commercials, as a writer, and as a producer/executive for the music industry.

I have struggled with being in and out of the Christian sub-culture since I was a teenager. For the most part I am operating outside of the subculture. But when I work in the subculture, I take great pains to make sure that my work isn't readily available in the primary culture.

The problem is that for the most part, work within the Christian subculture is easier to come by and pays better. But if you accept it and do high-profile work within it, it will kill your chances of being accepted outside of the subculture. For example: If you are an anchor for the *700 Club,* like Lee Web, could you someday have the opportunity to host the *CBS Evening News?* Highly unlikely, unless you were to renounce your beliefs. It's not overt bias, it's just the way the world works right now.

I once passed up a chance to host a Christian television show, and a few years later I was hosting a mainstream TV show that had a few million more viewers. In this position I had the opportunity to shape the message and be salt and light. Still, I don't shun the subculture altogether. If you can spend some time bringing the subculture along and at the same time be salt and light in the mainstream, I think that's the best of both worlds.

I am an enthusiastic fan of strategic compromises so long as they don't involve moral compromise. A strategic retreat in war, for instance, doesn't mean you give up the war, but that you retreat to fight another day. There are times when that is necessary. The trick is to learn the difference between moral compromise, which is evil, and strategic compromise, which is not. I was once offered what I would call a moral compromise when as a teenager I went to an audition for a commercial and was told my role involved placing my hands on a woman's breasts. I passed. On the other hand, I accepted a strategic compromise that came my way when I was a reporter. I reported on less-than-moral artists in order to also report on artists who were believers, thus helping advance these believers' careers in the mainstream.

We are so obsessed with having clean hands, when in reality we all have dirty hands. I once asked Paul Jackson Jr., a guitarist who is a Christian but plays on a variety of recordings, what he thinks about this. I asked him what his rule is when asked to play on recordings made by bad people. He said he has only one rule: Pray and ask God what I should do. He could have boycotted Madonna's requests to play on her recordings, but what would that have accomplished other than depriving Madonna of contact with one of God's agents in the world? Is he any less responsible for furthering evil in the world than is the plumber who fixes Hugh Hefner's house and enables Hefner to continue his evil work?

These are questions that don't have easy answers, but need to be debated. In general, I think Christians should be everywhere and anywhere (though probably not in porn films) so long as they are of strong enough constitution to not let their surroundings move them or shape them in any way. That is the lesson of Daniel: If one's beliefs are unmovable, God will be able to trust you in situations and places where he can use you mightily among people who hate God.

I'd like to be remembered as someone whose primary goal in life was to gain a hearing for God among people who otherwise had no interest in Him.

—Mark

Chapter Twelve

If There Were No Christian World

———— ❧ ————

On the Fringes

I never did ask the Jewish woman who needed her house painted if she ended up doing a deal with the Christian painter, but I have my doubts. She may not have had enough confidence in his painting skills to hire him, or she may have had enough dislike of Christians that she didn't want him around. What's unfortunate about that is that he may have been a good painter. Announcing himself as a Christian painter marginalized his talents and took away his opportunity to compete on the same level as other house painters in the area.

A general discrimination against Christians in culture has pushed to the fringes many Christians skilled in areas of leadership, art, and communication. Many could have had an impact on society as a whole but instead chose to limit their expertise to the Christian community. In his book *Rock and Roll Rebellion* Mark Joseph likens this loss to African-American baseball players with major league talent who for years languished in the relative obscurity of the Negro leagues due to racial discrimination.[1]

In the case of music, this can be seen every year at the Grammy Awards, where all Christian music is lumped into the category of gospel music and given an obscure award off camera. Joseph points out that no one nominated the Beastie Boys for a Buddhist music Grammy, Marilyn Manson for a satanic music Grammy, or the Osmonds for a Mormon music Grammy, and yet Jennifer Knapp, Jars of Clay, and Third Day were all nominated in 2001 for a gospel music Grammy. They are not even gospel artists in the purist sense of the term. Gospel music as a genre is commonly considered the kind of soul music an African-American choir would sing in church. And yet the Grammy Awards categorizes gospel music as all music of any style that comes from a Christian label.

One might even wonder if there is a reason for this. If the world can categorize talented artists who believe in the gospel, put them into a separate genre of music called gospel music, and keep that music out of the mainstream of influence, then faith can be successfully marginalized and minimalized. This certainly does not bode well for the gospel. If all Christian music is gospel music, then the gospel stays trapped in Nashville. It may get handed a token, non-prime-time Grammy or a cable network Dove Award, but that's about it.

What we really want is for people who like jazz to end up hearing jazz written and performed by people who know and love Jesus and have a view of the world that is impacted by the gospel. We want people who love film to encounter movies written and performed by people who know and love Jesus and have a view of the world that is impacted by the gospel. We want people who love novels to end up reading stories written by people who know and love Jesus and have a view of the world that is impacted by the gospel. We want people who like their house looking good in the neighborhood to end up with a house freshly painted by someone who knows and loves Jesus and has a view of the world that is impacted by the gospel.

Dropping the Label

What I am really saying here is that to have a significant impact on culture, Christians may have to drop the Christian label. Being good at something outside the realm of "Christian" will prevent the gospel from being marginalized and bring a Christian perspective into the general marketplace. This goes for all kinds of cultural expression, even the business world.

In an article in *Fortune* magazine titled, "God and Business,"[2] a number of successful Christians in business reveal how their faith impacts their work. Jose Zielstra is a high-level executive who, the article says, "has been able to live her faith at both Pricewaterhouse and JP Morgan Chase... by encouraging executives to look up from spreadsheets to focus on people and values, and by arguing for what's right, and by trying to act with compassion. She's guided as much by the Bible as by any corporate dictate or business school text." And yet, Zielstra has done this without trumpeting her Christianity. "On the job, Zielstra uses secular language and avoids the 'G' word (God)."

This is a unique and needed perspective. I must say I have encountered enough of the business side of the Christian subculture to know what it is to have secular values disguised in Christian language. How refreshing to hear it the other way around—to have Christian values disguised in secular language. What's more important, the values we hold or the language we wrap around them?

No Christian Subculture

Imagine, just for sake of argument, what it would be like if there were none of the Christian products and services available that support a Christian subculture. What if we all woke up one morning to discover that the entire industry that supports Christian merchandising had slipped into some black hole in the universe and disappeared forever. No Christian record companies. No Christian promoters of Christian events other than church. No Christian book-stores. No Christian schools. No Christian radio or television. What would the world be like? What would happen to all those Christian authors, singers, teachers, administrators, promoters, and business people who were making a living in the Christian subculture?

The simplest answer is they would either be out of jobs or they would find jobs in the general market. The most experienced and talented would be in the latter group. There would undoubtedly be a surge of Christian presence in some of the places of greatest cultural influence. And if this were done quietly, giving preference to the job done well rather than to one's Christian statement or witness, a long-lasting impact could be made on business and on society. I believe this is exactly what Jesus meant when he called us the salt of the earth (Matthew 5:13). He meant for us to spread out and take up positions in society as individuals, as opposed to being an army in attack mode. It's a long-term strategy of friendly infiltration, with God working through individual believers as they come into relationship with non-Christians.

Now of course the Christian subculture is not going to up and disappear any time soon. There is too much at stake. But imagining the world without it helps to envision the kind of influence we could have on society if we ignored the subculture. The more Christians we have taking up positions in the world as a conscious choice, the more we will be able to push back the darkness in our world.

Hilsen fra Norge!

Welcome to Norway, a country where, like most European countries, there is almost nothing cultural labeled as "Christian." To be sure, there are Christians in Norway, but not a subculture that shields them from the rest of the world. So if anything "Christian" happens on a scale big enough to be noticed, it's just thrown into the mix with everything else. For that reason, European countries such as this are an interesting study on how we might think outside our boxes when it comes to Christianity and culture.

Twice during the 1990s I attended a gospel music festival in Kragero, a lovely little seaside town on the southern coast of Norway. The festival enjoyed its twenty-first year in the summer of 2001. These were not Christian events as much as they were summer tourist specials supported by the whole town. The locals have come to trust the good weather that seems to always accompany the festival, so much so that they plan their weddings and private parties accordingly, figuring these gospel people have an inside track on whoever controls the weather. It reminds me a little of pagan nations in the Old Testament that never embraced the God of Israel, but didn't take any chances stepping across his path just the same.

In Norway, there doesn't appear to be the same kind of cultural separation we are accustomed to in America separating what Christians are doing and what the rest of the world is doing. The music at these festivals is mostly created and performed by Christians, but it is accepted at face value by the audience, many of whom are not Christians. They come because they like the music. They come because they recognize a good thing when they hear it. They even come to patio bars in town late in the evening and listen to American born-again blues, even listen to the gospel being openly preached in and around songs as they step in and around a few non-listeners passed out on too much stout Norwegian ale.

I wonder if we have come to expect too much from this kind of event in America. Somehow we are not willing to stop at just having a joyous celebration of believers to which unbelievers are welcome. We must get people to come forward, get down on their knees, and get changed, healed, and filled. Then we send them out, all in one evening. In Norway, it's enough for Christian artists to be talented and to present themselves in an honest manner as men and women who enjoy their work. In America, a Christian artist must also be a minister and a preacher who is capable of producing on-the-spot spiritual results.

During this event, the population of Kragero will double, and yet there will be no complaint from the townsfolk. They are, in fact, abuzz with excitement over their burgeoning little town. This gospel music fest—Sklaergardsgospel—is good for business and a boost to civic pride and morale.

Contrast this with the United States, where Christians descending en masse upon a poor unsuspecting town would usually be met with a different reaction. That's because American Christians are traditionally unfriendly to locals (unless they are witnessing). They don't drink, they order the cheapest things on the menu, they make unreasonable demands on the service, and they rarely tip. And a large group of Christians together has a tendency to heighten these negatives. Believing there is strength in numbers, they see themselves in enemy territory, but their numbers make them bold. The result can be unpleasant for some.

So what makes American festivals so different from a similar event in Norway? I can think of at least four things: a subculture that separates Christians from the world, a theology that makes them enemies with the world, a prejudice that makes them better than the world, and an industry that propagates these ideas and impressions. Experiencing Norway has given me just a taste of what our society might be like without a Christian subculture, and it isn't so bad.

Just a Phase

As much as I like to have this discussion, it always makes me personally uneasy, because it shows a certain inconsistency in my own position. This very book, which advocates living beyond the walls of a subculture, probably wouldn't be in anyone's hands without it. Not to mention that my livelihood comes from the Christian subculture. If everyone did what I advocated, I would be out of a job. This is somewhat disconcerting.

The truth of the matter is: The Christian subculture is here to stay—at least for the time being—and yet it is not necessarily for all believers for all times. Just as babies and young children need looking after, new Christians need protection. They are at a time of tender faith. That faith needs care to grow and develop. But just like a baby moves from milk to solid food, a believer moves to maturity, with discernment. Thus it could be said that the Christian subculture may be a phase some people pass through. There is a time in one's walk as a believer when all this Christian stuff is pretty cool. New Christians are amazed to find how many believers there are in the world and how many helps are available to foster one's growth as a believer.

This is why I believe that the Christian subculture will always have a steady flow of traffic traveling through it. It may serve a valuable purpose in the beginning of one's Christian walk. The concern comes when a person remains in a dependent relationship with the subculture long past the time when he or she should be spiritually mature and able to handle the word and the world on the person's own. This is no more attractive than seeing a 17-year-old in diapers.

In the meantime, it can't hurt to think about what you would write, speak, and do outside the walls.

No Christian World

So what if there were no Christian world? It would sure simplify things. It would pretty much take care of safe, easy faith. You wouldn't be a Christian unless you really meant it, because it wouldn't be safe to be one. You would have to learn how to speak about your faith on your own, because there would be no cultural entity speaking for you. You would have to learn how to find God in the world, since there would be no separate Christian world where he (and you) is hiding out. And since you know he's "at large," you would have to learn how to find him and introduce others to him. You would have to learn how to let your life, and whatever it is that you do, speak for itself. You would have to be whatever it is that you are, do whatever it is that you do, and be a Christian on top of that—and a Christian through and through. There would be no label, no T-shirt, no hat, no bracelet, no insignia—just you and your faith.

Sounds pretty good to me. Sounds like the way it should be. Perhaps if we lived as if we didn't have a subculture, we would begin to have a better, more lasting impact on the world.

"Pop-Culture Christianity"

Trygve is a chaplain at a Christian College in the Midwest.

I am fiercely uncomfortable with the evangelical subculture. I am at odds with the values of this subculture because I think they are at odds with Jesus. We are not critical enough of the culture that we live in. We think culture is neutral. We think that we can live in our environment and not be affected as we seek to win it for Christ. But we are wrong. Nothing is neutral. We cannot expect to borrow every device and idea and twist them for Jesus' sake and still come out clean. We must be honest about the fact that ours is a shallow culture. If we are set on capitulating to it, we will inevitably reflect its lack of depth.

We must work harder at discerning where we stand. We need to take a hard look at American culture, at its values and its appetites, and compare it with the kingdom Christ bids us to join.

Many of us in America have a vested interest in seeing this system protected and maintained, and we have lost any kind of prophetic edge to call the powers to faithfulness toward God. We like the way things are because we get lots of cool stuff. What has happened, however, is that we are slaves at the altar of secular rhythms that celebrate consumption over creation, stimulation over silence. We are people living tired and thin lives as we race over concrete to make our next appointment.

I feel alienated because I come from part of an evangelical ethos that prevents us from knowing what I am lamenting. I am frustrated because this same culture is now part of the problem I am trying to articulate. If we, the evangelical community, are to take forming souls seriously we need to refashion an evangelical identity. We must repent of the desire to be relevant in order to offer revelation. We need to stop following fad and fashion in order to experience faithfulness.

I hate the encouragement to be "relevant." If the culture is polluted I don't want to be relevant. I want to clean it up. Doctors are not relevant to cancer; they cut it out before it spreads and kills the entire body. We need to create space and time for what is most important: worship, prayer, hospitality, study, and service. We must be an alternative people with a gospel imagination.

I am finding that there are a lot of people who think as I do, but we are not easy to box or categorize. We are those on the fringes of the evangelical culture—living on the margins of the church—almost invisible. We feel discarded, ignored, and misunderstood. We are seeking to sink our roots deeper into the soil of the faith. We want an alternative to the dominant culture. We do not fit into prefabricated structures of pop-culture Christianity, a gospel of moralism, or the triumphant enterprise to save culture through education, legislation, or social programs. Instead of wanting to save culture, we want a savior. Instead of moralism, we want wisdom.

We have difficulty wearing the placated smiles of the evangelical culture. We are not always happy. We get angry and don't hide it well. We suffer from rough edges. Sometimes we have a drink (or two), and you may find one of us smoking, or even swearing in frustration. This may seem offensive, particularly if those still learning how to control angst with tact are unaccustomed to it. But don't misread the energy in the lament or the acts of social rebellion. We get mad, but we have not left the building. We simply want to be taken seriously. Sometimes you have to be mad in order not to be seduced.

—Trygve

Chapter Thirteen

Get Smart

*The years since Mark's death have flown by, but the
emptiness is still here. It is helped tremendously, however, by many young people with intelligence, great
spiritual insight, and the ability to communicate
their faith with freshness and originality.*

—Mark Heard's mother

Richer by Sixpence

We need to be smarter about our witness in the world.
Following on the heels of their hugely successful 1999
single "Kiss Me," the Christian rock group Sixpence None
the Richer appeared twice on *Late Night with David Letterman*. On their second visit, David Letterman decided to
give lead singer Leigh Nash a brief interview after the group's
performance on the show. It was a rare opportunity for a
Christian to be in the cultural hot seat, so to speak, and
Leigh handled it deftly. When asked about the meaning of
her band's name, she brought up the popular English writer
from which the name came.

"It comes from a book by C. S. Lewis," she said. "The book is called *Mere Christianity*. A little boy asks his father for a sixpence—which is a very small amount of English currency—to go and get a gift for his father. The father gladly accepts the gift, but he also realizes that he's not any richer for the transaction because he gave his son the money in the first place."

"He bought his own gift," Letterman clarified.

"That's right. Pretty much," replied Nash, with a sheepish grin. "I'm sure it meant a lot to him, but he's really no richer. C. S. Lewis was comparing that with his belief that God has given him and us the gifts that we possess, and to serve him the way we should, we should do it humbly, realizing how we got the gifts in the first place."

"Well, that's beautiful," David remarked to an overwhelming audience response. "That's very nice...Leigh Nash, ladies and gentlemen...charming!"

In a few brief minutes on national TV, Leigh Nash accomplished an incredible feat probably without knowing she was doing anything but being herself. She was an example of humility in a position that usually is accompanied by arrogance, and she cast belief in God in an intelligent and creative manner.

"It's awesome! Just...all my dreams are being fulfilled," she said, when David pressed her over the group's sudden success. His attempt to jokingly turn Leigh's enchantment into a clandestine hotel tryst was met with an innocent response that betrayed the singer's genuineness.

"I'm being needlessly coarse. I'm sorry," was all David was able to muster in an attempt to regain some dignity, and the audience loved it. The people couldn't help but respond from some authentic place in their own souls. Bashfulness is a rare and welcome commodity in today's satiated society.

A few minutes on David Letterman's show may not seem like much, but in light of the media's relentless stereotyping of Christians, it was significant. We can go a long way by merely being real Christians in the world. And if even for a brief moment the mere Christianity of our lives can be put on display, it will, by its very nature, disarm many false perceptions and cause some folks to have second thoughts about Jesus Christ.

Leigh Nash may have had her moment on national television, but the rest of us will have similar moments of equal importance around the water cooler, while carpooling, at our kid's baseball game, or when chatting with our neighbors. Anywhere we encounter non-Christians, we do battle with a stereotype. This is why we need to be smarter about our witness in the world.

Can You Keep a Secret?

I've heard it from Christians in music and in the arts. I've even heard it from some pastors. Now I'm hearing it from some of my friends. "I'm a Christian but I really don't want anyone to know it." Could such a statement ever be right? What about being bold and standing up for your faith and all that? Isn't someone who says something like this admitting he or she is ashamed of the gospel?

Well, I know the people who have told me things such as this, and they are not ashamed of the gospel. And I know myself pretty well, and I tend to agree that given the present cultural situation, this is a time when one might best serve the cause of the gospel by keeping quiet, at least initially, about one's faith.

When would it ever be right to keep your Christianity a secret? When you know that the people around you who are not Christians have the wrong idea about it. Unless you want to wear a pin with "I'm a Christian but don't hold that against me" on it, or "I'm a Christian, but I'm not one of them," you probably don't want people to know about your faith without first establishing with them a relationship of trust and mutual respect. The message will be coming soon enough; first you'll want to establish a connection based on our common humanity. We live in a strange time—a time when our Christianity might actually keep someone from knowing Christ. Unless we make some kind of human connection with non-Christians, they may listen to us for a while, but they will soon tune us out, leaving us in the clouds where they think we belong.

Taking a Stand

To speak of having a fearless faith would seem at first to indicate a bold testimony in the face of opposition. As a child in Sunday school, I was always inspired by the stories and testimonies of those who took a stand for their faith. Not drinking at a party, not going to the dance, not running with the crowd—these were the exploits of the fearless Christians among us. "Taking a stand" always had to do with some behavioral code that set us apart from everyone else. It heralded a faith that laid it all on the line. Well, this may have been fine for Martin Luther or the martyrs, but in today's social climate of political correctness and post-modern relativism, such a stand is usually meaningless at best. It rarely translates into what we think it does. It may represent our faith and practice, but it means little to those who can't possibly have the same perspective as we do.

Taking a cultural stand in society today may often make us look like supporters of a static faith, one that wants to go backward rather than forward; a faith that longs for the bygone days when "this-far-and-no-further" ultimatums meant something. It looks like a memorized faith rather than an internalized one. It hits and runs. It is all words and separation. I am not so sure it is the words that are needed now as much as the touchable, everyday expressions of the gospel that come through human hands, heart, and conversation. We need to be connecting with the world, not separating from it. We need to build bridges to our culture, not create fault lines.

More than ever, we need to get down and *be* the gospel instead of just standing up for it or talking about it. This is where a fearless faith trusts the Holy Spirit to do his work with the meager offerings we bring. Not every question has to be answered. Not every error has to be corrected. Not every truth has to be told. God knows how much is enough. If it were all up to us and our grand powers of persuasion, we would have cause to fear. But our faith is fearless because it does not depend on us. It's fearless faith that can walk away knowing there is an interpreter—that God is tugging on people from the inside, that God has his own invisible cords connected to their hearts, that there is a voice from within to echo our voice from without and confirm the truth, that deep calls unto deep, and some of it is deeper than our own consciousness.

It's a fearless faith that can set someone off on a search in any direction and know that God will direct their steps to himself. A fearless faith goes both ways. It gives and receives. It learns and teaches. It recognizes the gems of truth as all cut from the same stone. It does not demand correct interpretation and all the right words. It looks for the meaning behind the words more than the words themselves. It primarily demands honesty and a broken heart.

We need to be smarter about our witness in the world.

Some people today reject Christianity simply because it's Christian and they are predisposed against Christians. They may be turned off to Christianity but still open to truth. People can reject Christianity and still accept Christ, but it's going to take someone they respect to show them the difference. Chances are, it will be someone they didn't realize was a Christian until, we hope, it's too late and they have to like them anyway and give their faith a closer look.

The message is not just words. People contain the message in their hearts. We are bearers of Christ. A life is usually the most powerful message, and a broken one is even a better carrier than a perfect one. In the past, I think we have erred in making the message and the image more important than the real life behind it.

Dazzling Gradually

Tell all the truth but tell it slant—
Success in circuit lies.
Too bright for our infirm delight
The truth's superb surprise.
As lightning to the children eased
With explanation kind,
The truth must dazzle gradually
Or every man be blind.
—EMILY DICKINSON

This poem by Emily Dickinson makes two important points about a Christian's witness in the world. First, coming to an understanding of truth is a circular process, and second, God shows us his glory a little bit at a time. All those Christian speakers were wrong when they tried to put a guilt trip on us by making us think that our words to someone might be the last chance God has to save them. Success comes in circling back to the same truth over and over, seeing it from a different angle until we get it. That's the process by which God teaches us. He doesn't give it to us all at once and then stand there waiting for our decision. God parcels his truth out little by little, and each time around we get more of an understanding of its depth and breadth.

Not only does he take his time with this, but his nature is to hide himself and send us on a search. "It is the glory of God to conceal a matter; to search out a matter is the glory of kings" (Proverbs 25:2). God has been playing hide and seek with us all along. I believe this process represents his joy in the interaction. He finds glory in concealment; we find glory in the search. To dump all the truth we know on someone all at once is to ignore the delicate process by which God draws people to himself.

We need to learn from Jesus, who told stories when his listeners wanted specifics—stories about farmers and merchants and workers in the field. And when it came to his own story, he lived it more than he told it. He lived it while everyone watched.

We need to learn from Jesus, who never gave interviewers a straight answer. When they asked him questions, he questioned them back. He put words in their mouths. He made them answer their own questions. He made them responsible for finding what they were looking for, though they were never very far away from it. No one is. He told them that if they were to see and hear the truth, they would need different eyes and ears for it than the ones they were born with.

God has reasons for hiding. He doesn't put himself on display for just anyone. This hiding of the fullness of his truth is a vital part of his glory. God is so big and vast and glorious that it is ridiculous to think that we could capture him, explain him, see him, or understand him fully. God finds glory in concealment for the same reason no one can look at his face. If we could assimilate his glory, we would have to be his equal. And we are not. We are only dazzled, at best.

The kind of involvement God exercises in our process of coming into a relationship with him is far from demeaning to us. Quite the contrary. It shows how God respects us—his own creation—and involves us in the process of discovery. What's more, he asks us to learn from this and treat others accordingly. "Do not give dogs what is sacred; do not throw your pearls to pigs. If you do, they may trample them under their feet, and then turn and tear you to pieces" (Matthew 7:6). Some people get it and some people won't. Now, given the fact that we are not always good judges of people, it would seem to me that carefully chosen opportunities and a gradual revealing of the truth of Christ in our lives would give us some indication of the current state of someone's openness to hearing it. This, at least, is how I understand Christ's unusual words about dogs and pigs. Don't tell everybody everything. If God parcels the truth to us, we need to do the same thing for others. This, I believe, is the sense and the truth of Emily Dickinson's poem.

We need to be smarter about our witness in the world.

Character Counts

In the mid-1990s, Jason Alexander, co-star of *Seinfeld* and numerous films, gave a commencement address at

Boston University's School for the Arts. I have been carrying around a quote from that address ever since.

> I am famous. That is a large part of why I was asked to speak here today…It is a large part of the reason I received an honorary doctorate today when in fact I don't even have a bachelor's degree—because I'm famous. I would like to think that it's also because I'm a pretty good guy, and I'm passionate about my craft and my business, but it's not. It's because I'm famous, and the funny thing is that my fame is a complete accident…Fame, this thing that I have, is very rare, very strange, and very meaningless. It's a poor measure of success…Look beyond the veneer of what you consider success. I would like you to try to focus now and for the rest of your lives not on glory, but on greatness.

Glory versus greatness is the key distinction here. Greatness has to do with character; glory has to do with fame. I believe that as Christians we have tried to grab the spotlight for the sake of the gospel and gotten blinded by the lights. The fact that Christians are now better known (more famous) in society and the media than we were 20 years ago hasn't necessarily been as good for the gospel as we had hoped. In some cases—as with those who have been blinded by the spotlight—it has been detrimental to the gospel.

I think that for a while we were naive enough to think that all that mattered was getting a Christian on stage, or getting a Christian on television, or getting a Christian into the top ten hit songs, or getting a Christian on the cheerleading squad, or getting a Christian in the White House. The rest would be automatic. Because a famous person was a Christian, we assumed everyone would suddenly admire

Christianity and want to be a Christian. How wrong we were.

Where the world is concerned, we need to focus more on greatness than on glory. Greatness involves serving humanity. As Christians, we often forget that in being a member of the family of God, we have not given up our citizenship in the family of man. We are citizens of the earth and as such have a responsibility to the planet and all the people on it. True greatness is not only greatness in a Christian subculture, but is also a greatness that translates outside that subculture to the world at large.

Greatness is realized over time; fame is fleeting. Though there will be some people who possess both greatness and fame, more often than not, the two are not juxtaposed. Fame eats away at greatness. It tarnishes purity. Those who have maintained greatness amidst fame have been able to keep their minds set on goals other than their own celebrity.

Jason Alexander called his fame a "complete accident." I doubt many of us will be accidentally famous like him. I'm not sure we want to be, given the temptations and the skewing of reality that so often occurs. But greatness is attainable by everyone, since it has to do with inner character, service, and consistency.

Christians need to be people of whom it can be said that their neighborhood, their community, their world is a better place because they are in it. That kind of witness *is* helpful to the gospel. Character lends credibility to the gospel we represent; fame confounds it.

"Those Evangelical Christians..."

Debbie is an English teacher and administrator in a Christian college. The following comments are in relation to a national conference on college-level composition and communication where she presented a paper and received kudos for her research.

At a recent conference, I found myself in the company of five Native American researchers who were all lesbians. Only one of them knew I was a Christian. We were having lunch together when one of the women asked, "What made you choose Native American studies—you being white and all?" I smiled and began discussing my Cherokee heritage and my great-great grandmother, who had been a child during the Trail of Tears. At that she said, "Oh, I never knew. I'm sorry to have assumed otherwise."

The conversation soon turned to the biases these women encounter as women in the college classroom, as Native Americans, and especially as lesbians—a powerful three strikes if teaching in a regional university. The woman who knew I was a Christian turned to me gently and said, "Don't take this personally, but those evangelical Christians are the most bigoted, close-minded students I've ever encountered." I nodded in grim acquiescence to the truth of her observation.

Immediately someone else piped up with a look of absolute astonishment. "I didn't know your background was evangelical Christian." I smiled as coyly as possible and leaned into her, gently affirming her most dire fear, "Well, it's not just that my background is evangelical Christian, I am a practicing evangelical Christian." Her facial expression faded into devout perplexity. Then I added, "The key is how you define 'Christian.' I strive to honor and pursue a Christ-like life."

At that moment it was as if the Holy Spirit settled around our gathering. We talked openly about Jesus Christ, his teachings, the many misunderstandings between our two communities, and the utter beauty of Jesus' love for humanity. There we sat, six women, defined by our lifestyle choices (lesbian or Christian), all commonly facing persecution for our decisions, all delving into one another's hearts to gain greater insights into our likenesses rather than our differences. It was a liberating time that led to expanded understanding and genuine embraces—both physically and metaphysically.

This "luncheon of minds" underlies for me the importance of striving for excellence in a field rather than simply flashing the fish sign or WWJD bracelet to gain access. In my field, being a Christian is a huge disadvantage. Few scholars take Christians seriously. To be an effective witness, I must first situate myself as a peer.

I must confess that these women are not "projects" for me. My impetus for fostering relationships is not to "save" them. They are seekers much like myself. I value their companionship and the richness this brings to my life's journey as a follower of Christ. I believe it to be an atrocity to sidle up to others purely out of evangelical fervor. There must be a sincere, heartfelt desire to simply love others rather than to mold them into my idea of what they should be.

—Debbie

Chapter Fourteen

"It's Over; Go Home"

God and Ferris Bueller

What for me turned out to be a very prophetic statement in regard to today's Christian subculture comes from the high school hooky-playing antics of the character Ferris Bueller (played by Matthew Broderick) in the popular movie *Ferris Bueller's Day Off.* In this movie, while placating his clueless and adoring parents, Ferris successfully completes a fun-filled day away from school with his girlfriend and best buddy, much to the chagrin of his irate principal—who never catches up with him—and his fed-up sister—who can never prove him doing something wrong.

In the final scene, safely back in his bathrobe at home (he feigned sickness to stay out of school), Ferris smugly walks off camera to make a cup of tea in the kitchen. After all the credits have rolled and the movie studio emblem has appeared on the screen, Ferris suddenly reappears with cup and saucer in hand, lightly stirring the steaming liquid. With a puzzled look on his face, he walks straight up to the camera and says to whoever might still be watching, "What? You're still here? It's over. Go home."

As early as 1987, when I first saw this film, I recognized the significance of this statement as it relates to the growing Christian subculture in America. I can clearly say God spoke to me through this scene and Ferris Bueller's words. I realize it may seem suspect to some for God to speak through a less-than-exemplary character in a Hollywood movie, but that's the way God works in my mind. For after I saw the scene, I saw a vision of God appearing before, not a movie audience, but an audience that represented for me the entire Christian subculture, an audience enthusiastically applauding the end of yet another blessed Christian concert. The audience's hopes for an encore are dashed, however, as God himself, in a bathrobe, parts the closed curtain and saunters slowly out to the edge of the stage, stirring a cup of hot tea. I'm not sure how people in the audience know this is God, but they do. A hush falls over the shocked and dumbfounded crowd. Those in the audience were expecting neither God nor Ferris Bueller. They just wanted another song to take them one step higher. And then God speaks. "What? You're still here? It's over. Go home."

Show's Over

There are at least three parts to this simple message. The first part is as simple as the message: There is no reason to hang around when something is over.

The second part becomes more complete. What, exactly, is over? In the movie, it is the movie itself that is over. In my vision, it is some kind of Christian concert attended by a very large crowd of Christian people that is over. But on a deeper level, something else is over. The concert and its audience represent for me the co-opting of Christianity by those of us in the Christian subculture who are using Christianity for our own sake, not the sake of others. Christian stuff for Christian people. Something about that is over now.

But the irony is that the vision that brought me this understanding came to me at a time of unprecedented success in Christian retailing, and there has been nothing but exponential growth since. I have already quoted in this book two national news sources chronicling the growth of the Christian industry, and there seems to be no letup in sight. So just what *is* over, then, since it doesn't look like it's the Christian subculture?

I believe what is over is not the Christian subculture itself, but the subculture's effectiveness in the world at large. What began as a way of reaching a generation for Christ has turned into a private event for a growing number of Christian consumers who are looking for a safe spot in which to hide from a dangerous world. In this regard, it's been over for some time. It's been over since the whole direction of Christian enterprise turned inward to bless Christians instead of blessing the world with the gospel.

It's been ten years since I first saw the Ferris Bueller movie, and time has only served to underline the spiritual implications to me of Ferris's words at the end of the movie. All of the culturally expressed relevance of the gospel and biblical truth that we have taken such pride in for so long has made but a small dent in the world. And isn't that what our Christian subculture is for? I've heard people all the way from record company and radio station executives to artists and concert promoters justify their work as a way to reach the world for Christ. And yet, where is that world? The world is certainly not in a Christian concert crowded with Christians. Nor is the world even interested in the Christian subculture except to make money off it.

I believe that if we members of the Christian subculture were to take half the time and money we spend supporting our subculture and use that time and money to pay more attention to our unsaved neighbors, we would reach a whole lot more unbelievers than we are reaching now.

Even the "You're still here?" part speaks to our current situation. A large crowd of Christian people waiting for the next great thing to happen at a Christian concert is an accurate picture of a subculture eager for one more worship experience. We've been conditioned by performance after performance. We've been taken to great heights by the music and the singing. We want more. We paid for this. We want our money's worth.

Which takes me to the third part of the message, which is as simple as the first: We are a subculture of passive consumers who need to go home to the real world where we live.

Go Home

It's time to break up the party and send everybody home. Time to scatter and make our way out into the places in the world where our faith makes a difference. Time to break out of our own Christian media commune into other media communes via great writing, great journalism, wonderful movies, creative new TV shows, popular songs, stimulating university professorships, and believable politicians—professional people of all kinds who happen to be Christian, though our faith may not be the first thing people know about us.

Our address is here, in the world. Though it is temporary, with respect to eternity, for now it is where we live. It is our neighborhood, our housing development, our apartment complex, our workplace. It is the place where our Christianity rubs up against the real world. It is the place where you can't deal in Christian words because no one knows what they mean. It is the place where you have to deal in meanings and experiences and connect with shared human needs. You can't simply be a smiling Christian painter. You must be a painter who can put his faith in human terms to connect in a meaningful way with those unfamiliar with Christian words and phrases.

This world is where the lost are, and the heart of Jesus has always been with the lost. Just listening to his stories of the lost coin (Luke 15:8-10), the lost sheep (Luke 15:4-7), and the lost son (Luke 15:11-31) should make evident the heart of God. The kingdom of God has always been in the business of finding the lost.

The Christian subculture, on the contrary, seems more interested in taking the found and turning them into a business enterprise. In other words, while the shepherd is out trying to find that one lost sheep, a Christian cottage industry has set up a booming business in the sheep corral, marketing to the other ninety and nine. It's my hunch that the shepherd isn't coming back to the corral anytime soon, except to drop off a few newfound sheep and go back out for more.

We need to get back into the world where the lost are. The world is our address. We don't live on Christian Street anymore. We never did. There is no such address. It is only a way of thinking that makes us believe we are more Christian if we separate ourselves from the world. But we are Christ in the world and the world needs Christ. This is no time to sequester ourselves in a subculture

He's Already Out

We need not think that by leaving the subculture we are leaving God. God is already out of the box. In reality, we are just catching up with him. He and his messengers have always been outside the boundaries of existing religious establishments. John the Baptist and Jesus are the most obvious examples. (I wonder how many churches would find it necessary to courteously but strongly escort these rabble-rousers out of their assemblies should either one of them appear today.)

God doesn't need a subculture—even a Christian one— to speak for him. He has indicated clearly throughout history that if he can't find a man or a woman to speak through, he will use a donkey. If he can't find a donkey, he will use a bush. If he can't find a bush, a child can speak. If the children are silenced, then the rocks will cry out. Certainly this same God would not find himself limited to what we now label as *Christian* to make his presence known.

I often imagine being a Pharisee (I wish this were harder to imagine than it is), and I wonder what I would have thought of John the Baptist. How could anything of God come from a person such as this? Where did he go to church? Who was he accountable to? Why was he dressed like that? What was he so upset about? And then I wonder how many John the Baptists are probably out there right now, dressed in a postmodern version of camel's skin, crying in the wilderness—and not being heard for the same reasons the Pharisees couldn't hear (Matthew 3:3-7).

God is already out in the world, and he has his people there, too, although many of these people are difficult to recognize as Christian because their faith is not worn on their sleeves. I am reminded of Elijah lamenting to God about being the only prophet and all that, and I can imagine God telling him, "Relax, Elijah. What you don't know is, I have 7,000 people who have not bowed their knee to any idol." Now where do you suppose God was keeping those folks? And why didn't Elijah know about them? If we only knew who God has out there, I think we would all be surprised. These believers have a faith based on the inner realities and beliefs that transform one's character and are made evident in a natural, gradual way. Real Christians in the world tend to be quieter on the surface, but are more powerful over the long haul.

The concept that God is already out in the world is a challenge to some of our cherished justifications for a Christian subculture. It also explains why our Christian witness is often so ineffective. If God is here (in my subculture) and not over there (in the world), then I do not have to concern myself with God when I'm in the world. It's expected that he is not going to be there. This is very convenient for the lazy believer. I have to think of God only when I'm involved in Christian things, and what's more, I have a subculture to do some of my thinking for me.

This all changes if God is present in the world. We don't get to write the world off. The world is not as god-forsaken as we'd like to imagine. If God is in the world, then I have to be a Christian all the time. I am not excused from thinking about him and finding him in the course of my life in the world. It's the difference between being a part-time and a full-time Christian.

The fact that we set "Christian things" apart from "things of the world" is evidence of our inability, and perhaps even our refusal, to find God in everything. Don't we sometimes use this as our reason for going to church or to a Christian gathering: to get our focus back on the Lord—as if we all assume the world will take our focus off the Lord? But this need not be the case. If we look at the world and don't see God, it's not because he isn't there; we just haven't learned how to see him outside of the context where we are more used to seeing him.

We need to cultivate the art of listening for God everywhere and seeing him in everything. This is a mandate for all contemporary Christians. You can no longer put your trust in something with a Christian label (as if we ever should have), nor can you presume godlessness upon the absence of a label. God is up to something in our world, and he's outside the box.

No Enduring City

"It's over. Go home."

If the Christian subculture is no longer a factor in influencing the world for Christ, then it is time for us to go back home where we belong—back to our address in the world. It's a move away from safety, away from what's comfortable for us.

"Go home" tells me: Go back to where you live out your faith moment-by-moment, day-by-day. Go back to where you are a resident of the world—not isolated in a subculture, but a part of the wider culture.

"Go home" tells me: You and I are it. We are the witnesses of Christ in the world. Not a concert, not a recording, not a march or a television special, but a reliable, steady, burning light in our neighborhood, a light that even though it may flicker from time to time, stays lit.

> You are the light of the world. A city on a hill cannot be hidden. Neither do people light a lamp and put it under a bowl. Instead they put it on its stand, and it gives light to everyone in the house. In the same way, let your light shine before men, that they may see your good deeds and praise your Father in heaven (Matthew 5:14-16).

We were never supposed to be safely tucked away anywhere. We are supposed to be a city on a hill, a lamp on a stand.

Visible.

Vulnerable.

The first house my wife and I bought was on the side of a hill and had a view of the ocean, about a mile away. Though it was a great investment and a grand location, I always felt a little uncomfortable there—like a fish in a bowl that people could easily see. I would have preferred being tucked away somewhere, unnoticed. I realize now that there should be something similar in my feelings about my faith in the world. I should be a little uncomfortable in the world because, spiritually speaking, I *am* a city on a hill. People *can* look in and see my faith. If Christians are not feeling some discomfort about their faith in the world, I wonder if they might be covering their lamp and counting on a Christian subculture to represent Christ for them.

Isn't that what the Christian subculture has become? A hidden city? A covered lamp?

Pushing Back the Darkness

I heard some time ago about an unsuccessful attempt to create a large Christian medical complex in Tulsa, Oklahoma, that would combine medical science and the power of prayer. Imagine a hospital where all the doctors and nurses and orderlies and receptionists are Christians. Imagine how many Christians from all over the country would want to go there—a kind of Christian Mayo Clinic. But it wasn't to be. I don't know how far the idea got, but it never came to pass.

Why would such a good idea fail? Probably because God didn't think it was such a good idea. Why take all that witness and all that light and put them all in one building when they could be scattered across the country to places where there are hardly any Christian doctors and other medical personnel, places where the light can shine more brightly against the darkness?

Hide a whole city of Christian medical professionals in one place? Who would go there for treatment? More Christians, of course. Think of all those people leaving their places of influence and moving to Tulsa when they could be used so much more effectively where they are, patients included. All those Christians in one place dilutes the power. Remove one light from a crowd of lights and it will hardly be missed, but remove it from a place where it is all alone, and the darkness will rush in. Perhaps God wanted everybody to stay home, to stay scattered across the world where they belong, where they were already having a greater impact than they could have all in one place. He wants us all pushing back the darkness in our little places in the world.

Many Christians count too much on the comfort of a Christian environment for the maintenance of their faith.

They depend on the familiar surroundings of church, fellowship, and Christian activity to help bolster their faith, as if somehow they could get it by osmosis. They don't interact with their environment as much as they blend in with it. But faith does not seep through the skin. It begins in the heart, and it is strengthened by the challenges placed upon it by a real and complex world. Home is where we are a light in the darkness—a house on a rock in the storm, a lamp on a stand, a city on a hill. Christians grow by being in a place where faith is at risk. This is, in fact, what cultivates a fearless faith.

Out Where It's Dangerous

Real faith must be wrestled with before it becomes a personal possession. Oswald Chambers said, "Always make a practice of provoking your own mind to think out what it accepts easily. Our position is not ours until we make it ours by suffering."[1]

We live in a subculture where faith comes easily. We need more provoking and we need more provokers. That which has come easily—that which has not been tested—will go as easily as it has come, like the seed that falls on shallow ground and sprouts up but is quickly burned off by the first hot day. It's not an issue of losing one's faith as much as an issue of never having had it fully in one's grasp in the first place.

Too many Christians today are expecting too much from a Christian environment. Too many are finding refuge in a nonthreatening subculture that hands faith out in neat, pre-thought-out packages. Too many are comfortable with their faith when, in reality, it should be dangerous to believe.

Too few believers are doing their own thinking. Too few are wrestling with their faith in a hostile world, thus making their faith their own. Too many are uncomfortable with having a fearless faith in a world in which they don't belong—always having to defend it in the face of criticism and answer to it for themselves. Hebrews 13:14 says "here we do not have an enduring city," but to look at a lot of churches and the subculture we have created in the last 30 years, you would think an enduring city was just what we had in mind. In some cases, it looks like we are trying to create an empire when it should have been a tent.[2]

If you think of home as a Christian place, in the company and protection of other Christians, you might be tempted to think of it as more permanent than it is meant to be. A home in the world seems more temporary, and that is as it should be. In reality, we have no home here. This is only a temporary address.

A New Playing Field

The premise of this book has been to establish the idea of a fearless faith in a dangerous world. The assumption has been that the Christian subculture as we know it today is motivated mostly by our desire for safety and security in the midst of a hostile world. But an even graver danger than a hostile world has arisen. It is the danger of depending upon a subculture where we simplistically think a label changes everything. We buy into the mainstream culture, substitute the Christian label, and think the world has been sanctified because our labeled message is getting across. "The medium is the message," according to Marshall McLuhan. In other words, the medium speaks louder than the message.

For instance, in our subculture we market what is popular, but the fact that it is a Christian version of what is popular does not automatically exempt something from being idolatry. We market "hip" and "cool" just like the world does, but the fact that it is Christian "hip" and "cool" doesn't make it exempt from vainglory. We peddle consumerism, but the fact that these are Christian products we are marketing does not justify the hype and false embellishment that often goes with the territory.

Is Christian materialism better than secular materialism? What would Jesus do about all this Christian stuff? I'm not sure, but I bet he wouldn't wear a bracelet that asks that question.

It used to be that those who expressed a clear Christian message in their music or art were sacrificing a greater success that could be had more easily in the mainstream commercial market. But as the Christian market grows in size and influence, this "sacrifice" is becoming less and less a factor. More often than not, it now goes the other way. People can make huge profits in the Christian market with the right kind of music (praise and worship) or art (Thomas Kinkade prints) or books (*Prayer of Jabez*).

Now it is the Christians who shun the Christian subculture for the world's marketplace of art and ideas who find themselves at the greater risk. In other words, Christians can make more money more quickly and more easily in the Christian market than we can in the world's general market. The Christian market is more exploitable than the world market. Imagine the compromises to which this gives opportunity!

The success of the Christian industry raises issues never before faced in contemporary Christianity. In a subculture that is increasingly separating itself from the rest of the world, we are marketing Christian products for the money and the glory—the very things Christians have criticized the mainstream for pursuing. Success is success; money is money—the love of which can corrupt the one who "ministers" as easily as the one who "entertains."

How about the tendency to fill songs with tried and true formulas of Christian expression to ensure a bull's-eye in the Christian market? One doesn't even have to be a Christian to learn how to do this. For years a Christian public has accused Christian artists seeking a mainstream audience of watering down the truth. But is the manipulation of truth or the use of tried and true Christian messages to ensure success in the Christian market any less wrong?

I think it's time to acknowledge that the playing field has changed. The same old arguments and justifications for a Christian subculture no longer apply. Crossing over or staying put mean little in the new scheme of things. Unholy compromise can tempt those on either end of the field. And courageous sacrifice can distinguish Christians both in and out of the confines of a Christian subculture. So it turns out that deeply committed Christians can sing with integrity about falling in love, just as glory-seeking charlatans can sing about giving their hearts to Jesus. One has to be careful about these things.

New ways of measuring success and new goals to pursue are called for. Integrity, truth, honesty, and vulnerability will always be paramount. Regardless of Christian content, getting right things right has never been more important. We are in a time when the Christian subculture can be more dangerous than the world. It will take a fearless faith in order to mature where the dangers are more subtle.

Come Together

As I wrap up this book, my wife and I are planning a neighborhood party. We had one two years ago when we first moved in. We wanted to meet our neighbors and let them see what we had done to restore and upgrade our house, a little two-bedroom cottage in the village section of Laguna Beach, California. We were pleasantly surprised at the turnout.

We are confident we'll have a good turnout again. Two years ago our neighbors might have just been curious. Now, there is a new sense of community—and a new sense of need. Now more than ever, people seem to want to come together. The war on terrorism has unsettled many. Suddenly people want to go home, be with the ones they love, and reaffirm what's really important to them. I've heard of enemies being reconciled, lawsuits being dropped, divorces being canceled—all due to a different perspective on everything. This presents a great opportunity to be friendly. Our sense of national safety is gone, and people want to go home and gather around them those who are close. For this reason, we are confident our neighborhood will come to our home again. They need us. We need them.

Is this evangelism? Is this a witnessing tactic? No. This is just a neighbor being a neighbor.

"Finding the Metaphor"

Noel is a performer whose platform has always been in the world, though for a brief period of time, he recorded albums within the Christian subculture after his conversion in the late '60s.

There's no question that personal expressions of faith are many times better understood by the Maker than by the faith community. Perhaps if I could have more easily accepted and used the inner language of the Christian community as my own, my career would not be viewed by so many as "out" in the world.

When I went through a glorious rebirth process in the late '60s, I was like a baby. I was happy, in many instances, just to have a goo-goo or a gurgle to express my joy at having been forgiven by a God who knows me personally. But the stronger I became in my faith, the less faith I had in using other people's terms for my relationship with the Divine. I think that smacks of being a bit unrepentant to some, but like I said, it's part of the balance I see between the sharing of faith with community and seeking a deeper personal relationship with God.

I seldom measure my Christianity in the context of organized religion. My devotional times are pretty much spent creating a prayer chapel in the shower every morning, practicing forgiveness and thankfulness daily, and going to God in even the small daily decision-making, especially in the prioritizing of duties and responsibilities.

The greatest challenge to me is to find the bridging words—the language to retain the integrity of my faith without resorting to clichés. But I love the challenge. The principles of God's truth are so monumental and so timeless that it's really more often a question of finding the metaphor that describes the mutuality of belief than it is "defending the faith."

—Noel

CHAPTER FIFTEEN

Evangelism 101

—————————— ✍ ——————————

Flunking Witnessing

My pastor tells a story about a classmate of his in Bible college who flunked witnessing. It was an actual class on witnessing—probably something like Evangelism 101. His classmate flunked because she didn't have a testimony.

The whole point of this class was to develop your personal testimony so that you could later use it as a basis for your own evangelism. Apparently she flunked the course because she could only talk about how she was "in the process of coming to faith in Christ." Her testimony was too incomplete and too present tense for her to pass Evangelism 101.

The idea behind this approach to evangelism is a popular one. You start with a somewhat gripping story of how you became a Christian, and then you hone it until you get it down pat. Most testimonies have the same general format: You tell what brought you to your conversion, how miserable and sinful you were before, and how happy and much better a person you are now. Once you have this story down, you memorize it, rehearse it, and practice it on fellow classmates until it is second nature to you. Only then are you ready to go out on the street and share your testimony with real people.

Jesus had something quite different to say about witnessing. "On account of me you will stand before governors and kings as witnesses to them…do not worry beforehand about what to say. Just say whatever is given to you at the time, for it is not you speaking, but the Holy Spirit" (Mark 13:9-11). It looks as if Jesus' disciples might have flunked witnessing, too.

It's a God Thing

It would save a lot of trouble and embarrassment if we could learn one simple thing about witnessing and evangelism: Salvation is God's thing and is out of our control. Saving people is God's part, ours is being a witness.

It's not up to us to tie the knot, close the deal, or keep our foot in the door. We are not salesmen. We are not headhunters. We are not on a crusade. We are witnesses to what we have seen and what we know. We tell our story, but it shouldn't be a rehearsed one. We tell the story from whatever page we are living it on at the time—and God does the rest. The teacher of Evangelism 101 didn't think my pastor's classmate had enough of a story to go out witnessing with, but God could have used her quite well right where she was, perhaps even more powerfully than her classmates who passed witnessing, because her story would have been more real, less polished, and "in process"—just like life.

Most of us don't seem to trust God enough in our approach to evangelism, and I believe this is a cause of unsolicited grief for unbelievers and unnecessary guilt for Christians.

One of the most heralded passages on evangelism, which I'm sure has sparked numerous worldwide mission efforts, is found in Paul's letter to the Romans.

> "Everyone who calls on the name of the Lord will be saved" (Joel 2:32). How, then, can they call on the one they have not believed in? And how can they believe in the one of whom they have not heard? And how can they hear without someone preaching to them? And how can they preach unless they are sent? As it is written, "How beautiful are the feet of those who bring good news!" (Romans 10:13-15).

Indeed. And yet in the very next breath, Paul says, "But not all the Israelites accepted the good news...Did they not hear? Of course they did" (Romans 10:16-18). And then he boldly quotes Isaiah, "I was found by those who did not seek me; I revealed myself to those who did not ask for me" (Romans 10:20). In other words, people's response to the gospel and our sharing of the gospel are not necessarily related. God is the key to the equation. People can't believe without hearing, but they can't hear unless God opens their ears. Preaching only guarantees he has a chance to do that; it doesn't guarantee he will. That's why coercion, manipulation, threats, or emotional badgering are not befitting the gospel. They are unnecessary. People's eyes and ears are either open or they are closed, and God has not given us as much as a clue as to how to pry them open. That's because saving people is God's job and being a witness is ours.

Raiders of the Lost Souls

The word "witness" in the New Testament is almost always used as a noun. "You will be my witnesses" (Acts 1:8) said Jesus. That's a far cry from going out witnessing—our common use of the term as a verb. Think of how we use the word. "Did you witness today?" "I witnessed to three people at work." "Are you witnessing for Christ or are you keeping your faith to yourself?" "Your problem is you need to get out and witness more."

In the interest of a more biblical understanding of this, I would like to suggest we at least take note when we use the term as a verb. Most of the errors involving witnessing show up in its use as a verb. Using the word as a noun is almost always more true to what the Scriptures talk about on this subject.

When witnessing is a verb it becomes something we do or don't do. We turn it on or we turn it off. It becomes a segment of the spiritual compartment of our lives, as in prayer, Bible study, going to church, and witnessing—a very small segment, I might add, in that it is a sub-compartment of a compartment. It's something we are supposed to go out and do, and poor, unsuspecting non-Christians often have to bear the brunt of our spiritual obligation. Witnessing, in this sense, involves tactics, methods, training, and planning. It tends to make us goal-oriented, opening the door to results, expectations, and, ultimately, the numbers game. With witnessing there are corners of cards to tear off, hands to raise, numbers to tally, reports to make. Witnessing is all one-way. *We* witness. *We* talk. *We* say what we came to say and try and make people listen to us. Such witnessing can have only two results: You either "pray the prayer" or you don't. And in the end, our witnessing can be judged as a success or a failure based on one response in one point of time. It has little to guarantee about the rest of one's life.

If I were teaching that class on Evangelism 101, I would write all these negative impressions of witnessing on the blackboard, and I'm sure the class would come up with many more to add. In no time, the board would be full. I would probably be squeezing things into tiny, unused spaces. Finally, when there was simply no more room, I would erase the entire board and write one thing in its place: "You shall be my witnesses," and nothing more would need to be written down.

"You Shall Be My Witnesses"

What is the difference between witnessing (the verb) and being a witness (the noun)? A witness is someone who has seen something and tells what he or she saw when called upon. It is someone who has experienced something and relates a story about what was experienced.

Here is a wonderful, guilt-crushing truth: *Every witness is an expert.* No one is more informed on what you have experienced with Christ than you are, simply because no one else can be you. No class, seminar, or workshop can teach this. Your witness is your own present tense, your continuing story, and no one but you can tell it.

When we stick with an honest telling of our story as our spoken witness, we are guaranteed a connection with others on a human level. As long as our story is told mostly in the present tense—relating the current ways in which we are experiencing God's grace, forgiveness, and power—our witness will be as effective as it needs to be.

Keep in mind that a witness (the noun) is not always witnessing (the verb), at least verbally. In the courtroom, for example, witnesses don't tell their story until they are called up to the stand. Even so, they are listed as witnesses before they are put on the stand. They are considered witnesses whether they are in the process of telling what they saw or not. If they are key witnesses (in legal terms), they may even be put under court-ordered protection to ensure they get a chance to tell their stories. Likewise, many Christian witnesses in key places of influence are careful to use their positions wisely. They wait until they know their story will mean something or will get the proper hearing. In the meantime, they continue to be witnesses by the way they live their lives so that when they are called up to speak, their lives stand behind what they say. It's almost like a riddle: A witness is not always witnessing, but a witness is always a witness.

This is why being a witness (the noun) is so much more effective than going out and witnessing (the verb). Witnessing tends to be hit and run. It is sometimes even rude. We may tell our story to people who don't want to hear it and didn't even ask. Even if they don't mind hearing it, there may be no context to our story—no life behind it—if we are strangers to each other. Now to be sure, God can use this kind of witnessing—and does—but in a limited way compared to Christians who realize they are expert witnesses all the time by the way they lead their lives. I would venture to guess that people who go out and find success in witnessing (the verb) are in reality beholden to all those who went before them and were faithful witnesses (the noun) in the lives of the people to whom they themselves are now witnessing (the verb).

Another Kind of Invitation

Sharing our faith should involve an invitation. Not an invitation in the traditional evangelical sense of the word, where every sermon ends with a call to come forward and receive Christ. I am not talking about our invitation to non-Christians, but theirs to us. Such an invitation to share our life can come only reciprocally, after we have given someone our attention and respect.

Peter puts it this way: "Always be prepared to give an answer to everyone who asks you to give the reason for the hope that you have. But do this with gentleness and respect" (1 Peter 3:15). Peter is talking about the unbeliever's invitation to answer a question. An invitation to explain a hope. An invitation to give reasons for what we believe. Peter is implying a relationship of give and take with unbelievers—relationships with a history, just like Coleman Luck in his car with his non-Christian friend and fellow producer. These invitations are cultivated by friendships with our non-Christian neighbors. And this is the moment we wait for, when someone calls us up to the witness stand and questions us. But this rarely happens unless someone feels safe around us, regardless of what they believe.

I'm sure this is why Peter used those two words, "gentleness" and "respect." He's telling us how he wants us to go about communicating with non-Christians. "Gentleness" says, "I will not walk over you. I will not just wait for you to finish so that I can talk. I will not pass you by since you are not interested in what I have to say. I will not lose patience over your continual rejection of Christians or the gospel. I will be gentle with you because I am not the last line of defense for the truth.

"I do not have to correct everything you say that is wrong. I do not have to make sure you understand that what I'm saying is right. I am not responsible for your salvation, only for telling you, when you ask me, what I have experienced, so far, of Jesus Christ in my life."

Likewise, "respect" says, "You can be safe around me. I respect your right to believe whatever you want. It is not my goal to get you to agree with me. I respect your right to disagree. I respect your right to your own spiritual journey. I will not be threatened by your talk of 'other paths to God,' because I know in my heart that if you are seeking the true God, your path will lead you, sooner or later, to Christ. And if God can be patient with this process, so can I."

More Than One Way (to Jesus)

Many Christians operate under the belief that before we can get a person to believe in Christ we have to get them to disbelieve everything else. This is just not the case. There is some truth to be found in whatever a non-Christian is currently believing. When Paul spoke to the pagan worshipers and Greek philosophers in Athens, he started by commending them for being very religious people (Acts 17:16-34). In the midst of all their wrong thinking and unbelief, he still found something he could affirm. And he used this as the starting point for conversation. This is remarkable, especially when you consider that the people he was talking to were involved in atheistic philosophies, temple prostitution, and the occult. To be effective in our sharing, non-Christians should not feel that their beliefs are always under attack.

I once wrote a song with the chorus "Jesus is the only way, but there's more than one way to Jesus." Could someone get to Jesus by way of prostitution? Could someone get to Jesus by way of Buddha? Could someone get to Jesus by way of drugs? Could someone get to Jesus by way of murder? Could someone get to Jesus by way of Islam? I know or have heard of people who have traveled all these roads, and roads even more bizarre than these, to get to Christ. God wasn't absent from their lives before their conversion, was he?

We need to stop being threatened by other people's paths to Jesus. Some paths may be more direct, but almost any path will do if someone is earnestly seeking God. The Scriptures are very clear that if someone is seeking God with his whole heart, he will find him. The Scriptures also tell us that the only way to God is by way of Jesus, who is the way, and the truth, and the life (John 14:6). That means, then, that if people are earnestly seeking God, no matter where they begin, they will ultimately end up with Jesus. We don't have to invalidate an unbeliever's path and start them off all over again in another direction. We point them toward the next step.

In that same passage in Acts, Paul tells the Athenians, "God did this so that men would seek him and perhaps reach out for him and find him, though he is not far from each one of us. 'For in him we live and move and have our being.' As some of your own poets have said, 'We are his offspring'" (Acts 17:27-28). He spoke this way to a crowd of Greek philosophers and pagans, no less. He put God within their reach. In fact, God is almost breathing down their necks! They are that close.

> *Some are looking the other way*
> *When they really do want to meet Him.*
> *Some are going to be surprised to find*
> *There's no one there to greet them.*
> *He is the one who opens eyes;*
> *He is the one to close them.*
> *And the ones who thought they owned the key*
> *Will find that the door was open.*
> *Jesus is the only way,*
> *But there's more than one way to Jesus.*[1]

Sometimes I wonder if some Christians take more pleasure in keeping undesirables out of heaven than bringing them in. Sometimes we act as though that were the case. We are like the Pharisees whom Jesus condemned for guarding the door of the kingdom. "You shut the kingdom of heaven in men's faces. You yourselves do not enter, nor will you let those enter who are trying to" (Matthew 23:13).

Making It Count

The real tragedy in all this is that there are many Christians who do not even relate to unbelievers unless they absolutely have to. That's what has to change. We don't need to witness more, we need to relate more with non-Christians so that our witness will mean more. If our witness truly is more *who we are* than *what we do,* then we need to be in places where *who we are* makes a difference.

This is where being too entrenched in a Christian subculture can be detrimental to the gospel. The more time we spend with believers the less we are in the company of non-Christians. Some Christians act as if they have to *endure* non-Christians in their life, implying that the less they have to be around them, the better. I've even sensed from some that if it were possible to be surrounded by Christians all the time, that would be the most desirable. Desirable for us, perhaps, for our safety and comfort, but not for the gospel.

At the end of Christ's ministry on earth, he sent his disciples out as witnesses in the world. "You will be my witnesses in Jerusalem, and in all Judea and Samaria, and to the ends of the earth" (Acts 1:8). He was not talking about sending out evangelistic outreach teams here. He was not talking about short-term and long-term missions. He was talking about where his disciples would live their lives—scattered throughout the world as his witnesses. "You will be my witnesses" is not a command. It is a statement of fact. If there is any command implied in this statement it is a command to spread out where their lives would have an effect. "Stay here in Jerusalem until you receive my Spirit," he was saying, "then disperse yourselves all over the world where your lives, your faith, and your witness will make a difference."

There does not appear to be any choice in the matter. We will be his witnesses wherever we are. That's why he wants us all over the earth. This is why he prayed for us to be protected, because he knew we would be in danger.

After all, what good is it being a witness where everyone already knows?

"A Greenhouse Effect"

Mark, 46, is director of media services for a large church in the Midwest. As a missionary kid, he grew up in France and has spent considerable time there in mission work. Part of Mark's current job is to develop an advertising campaign for his church. An example of a slogan he is proposing: "Check your hat, not your brains, at the door." He is an ordained minister.

I've been just about everything there is to be in Christian radio, from DJ to general manager. I've been involved in the politics of it. I've attended the National Religious Broadcasters conventions. But I can hardly listen to it anymore. I feel the same way about walking into a Christian bookstore. There is so little that challenges the Christian to think about the outside world. It's all about us.

I honestly wonder if Christians even know or care that there is a real world out there beyond the walls of our subculture. We've become so ingrown. The French have a word for it: *nombrilisme,* which comes from *nombrille,* or belly button. You can probably figure it out from there. *Nombrilisme* is a philosophy of life where the whole world revolves around your belly button.

Many people in places of influence in the Christian subculture don't have a grasp of the sovereignty of God. It doesn't appear they believe God can minister directly to people, so they have to control everything. They're control freaks, directing people's lives instead of putting the truth out there and letting the Holy Spirit direct it.

It's a greenhouse effect. Christians stay trapped in a greenhouse, and no one gets planted in the world. We don't know how to talk to the unsaved. We are too full of ourselves. Statistics show that by two years after being saved, Christians have lost contact with unsaved friends on a regular basis. They're in a greenhouse.

I once carried out a mission in France that had me knocking on 4,000 doors and personally leaving people a card to fill out and send in for a free Bible and a study guide to help understand it. Know how many responses we had? Zilch, nada, nothing. If I were going to start another ministry there now, I know exactly what I would do. I would move into the neighborhood and love my neighbors. You've got to get the plants out of the greenhouse and plant them in the world where they can do some good.

We need to get the danger back into faith. We need more examples of Christians living out their faith in the world where it counts. I want a faith beyond what I've experienced so far. I want to be stretched. We should be willing to put up with anything instead of insisting everyone put up with us.

The great commission says "Go!" I would add: "...and don't come back!"

—Mark

CHAPTER SIXTEEN

Snapshots:
Fearless Faith in Action

————————— ✺ —————————

When I talk about fearless faith, I'm not just talking about an idea or an abstract concept. I'm talking about a way of living. Allow me to share with you a few snapshots of what fearless faith looks like in action...

Burning Down the Church

I knew I was in for a different experience when, arriving at the Minneapolis airport on a Saturday night to speak and sing in a church the next day, I was met by a buff, t-shirted man with tattooed biceps and turquoise and silver jewelry on both wrists. There is always a little tension when I arrive at baggage claim and search the faces of strangers for someone who might be searching for me. This man was coming straight for me, but I was sure he had mistaken me for someone else. Turned out this was only the first of many surprises. Thinking he was some new convert who had gotten roped into the airport assignment, I asked him how he had come to be the one picking me up. "I'm the pastor," was his immediate reply.

The next surprise came when he loaded my stuff into a Cadillac El Dorado he had borrowed from one of his church members because he didn't think there would be enough room in his Corvette for both of us and my luggage. There wouldn't have been.

As we made our way to the small lakeside town north of Minneapolis where he grew up and now pastors an Assembly of God church, I found out the 'Vette wasn't his only vehicle, nor was it his favorite. His love was his motorcycle, or maybe I should say his love was speed, in general, in anything fast enough to give him a thrill.

When his wife found out he was hitting 130 mph on the country roads outside their town, she had suggested that he look into racing. She was thinking it would at least be a little safer on a controlled track. Much to her dismay, he jumped at the idea. Turns out the only thing safer about racing is that emergency crews can get to you faster when you crash. Interesting tidbit: It is a requirement in motorcycle racing to have your name and your blood type on the back of your helmet.

The pastor raced for two years before he retired from that, happy to be alive. Over his office desk is a large painting by one of his church members of him leaning so far into a curve that his knee pads scrape the pavement. The picture from which the painting was taken is framed inside a motorcycle tire over the urinals in the men's room of the church. Other biker memorabilia adorns the bathroom including Harley Davidson parts and motorcycle wallpaper. Not your typical church men's room.

It doesn't take long to find out themes like this are common at this church. In the parking lot of their new building, there is a section marked off for bikers. The church is also famous in town for a car rally they sponsor every year which includes a popular contest to see who can burn the most rubber. Pastor Mike proudly pointed out the blackened pavement in a far corner of the parking lot as if he was showing me a trophy. Everybody in town knows about this rally. Many attend. Some are now Christians, and members of his church. There is also a wild game dinner, in season, when local hunters bring in their kill, and the church prepares a feast. Not to be outdone, the pastor's wife is now holding an arts and crafts show annually that is getting much attention in the community.

But by far, the most intriguing thing about this church was the story I heard of the demise of the previous building in which they met before they outgrew it. When he found out the building was going to be destroyed to make a parking lot for a strip mall, the pastor got an idea. First they gutted it of anything that was usable—furnace, light fixtures, doors, air conditioning unit—and donated them to a downtown church. Then they donated the shell of the building to the local fire department to be burned down as a training exercise. Pastor Haseltine loves to tell how the structure was able to minister to the public in its final hours by allowing firefighters a setting to hone their skills.

Maranatha Assembly of God Church in Forest Lake, Minnesota has a four-fold purpose: "To worship God, to draw people to Jesus, to teach and train, and to impact our community." And I have to admit, they're having lots of impact, and a lot of fun doing it. They're using what they have and what they love—hunting, crafts, cars, speed, motorcycles—and they are looking outward to their community, not inward to their safe isolation.

When word got out that the fire department was going to burn down the church, there were a number of phone calls to the fire department. The fire chief told the pastor that some of the men were getting concerned about burning down the "house of God." The pastor assured them that God didn't live in the building; he lives in our hearts. And then he prayed with the firemen on site before they set fire to the church. During the burning, a wall unexpectedly collapsed right before four men went in. They still credit their lives to that prayer.

Two O'Connors

Trying to define what is culturally Christian is an attempt to define the indefinable. Such would be the conclusion, at least, of American southern writer and Christian, Flannery O'Connor, were she alive today to comment. When asked to define a Christian writer, for instance, Ms. O'Connor was known to answer that a Christian writer is a Christian who writes about anything.

This simple statement shows that using "Christian" to define anything other than a person will always be problematic. Granted, the book you now hold is supported by an industry which includes a host of other Christian products and services that are impossible to talk about without using the term "Christian" to describe them. Yet merely calling something "Christian" doesn't make it somehow holy or set apart from anything else. It doesn't exempt it from error or worldly intrusion. Nor can we assume that something that does not carry the Christian label is *not* Christian by default.

This is often the unspoken assumption. It is simply not the case. This kind of perspective fails to comprehend the full realm of God's interest and involvement in the world.

This is why Flannery O'Connor's definition of a Christian writer as someone who writes about anything, is so helpful to us. It says two important things: 1) the term "Christian," in its truest sense, can only define a person, and 2) a Christian's faith applies broadly to anything a Christian does. In essence, "Christian" cannot really be a song, a television station, a bookstore, or a T-shirt. "Christian" is not a category; it is a person.

Using the term "Christian" for anything other than a person always limits the scope of God's presence in the world, and our responsibility to bring all things under His Lordship.

Many people don't know that Flannery O'Connor was a Christian. Her works, though they are few, are studied in virtually all institutions of higher education among important examples of great American literature. Many universities have upper level courses devoted to her writing alone. If the big deal about Flannery O'Connor was that she was a Christian writing Christian books, there is hardly a chance that she would be considered the writer that she is today — indeed, that she would even be known outside the circles of Christian publishing. But though her books are not "Christian," they are based on a Christian perspective on life, and in her case, on the innate depravity of human beings that colors even the most pious and religious among us. No one can read her stories and fail to encounter their own sinfulness and hypocrisy. Her stories strike something universal in all people, just like the truth always does. It is in this sense that her Christianity is bigger than "Christian."

A life committed to Jesus will always be bigger than any-thing Christian. That doesn't mean we lose all this Christian stuff. It just means we have to be wiser about what all of it means...and doesn't mean.

There is another O'Connor who is very alive today and writing, though not as famous in literary circles as Flannery. His name is Michael O'Connor and he is a friend of mine who has published a book titled *Sermon on the Mound*. As the title suggests, this book presents a strange and wonderful wedding of baseball and spiritual truth.

My interest in this book began when I met its author at a writer's conference and heard his preposterous claim that the failure of the Boston Red Sox to win the 1986 World Series in the sixth game when they had the New York Mets on the ropes is the reason why he is a Christian today. I won't even try to explain this since it took a whole book for him to do that, but I will say that I waited 12 years to find this out—12 years of suffering as a New England resident and avid Red Sox fan—never imagining that there might be another story to this unforgettable loss that would ease my pain.

If you think I'm crazy, that's fine, and to be expected. People don't generally go around consecrating major sporting events with someone's salvation experience, but then again, why not? Why couldn't something like this have occurred? Is God relegated to only saving people in church, at a crusade, or during an evangelistic canvassing of the neighborhood?

I think we keep God in a compartment because we are uncomfortable with having him out on the loose. We want to be able to control and validate everyone's spiritual expe-rience by some kind of set standard. We want God out of the world at large and involved only in Christian things so that we can justify their existence and reassure ourselves of our own spirituality. If God was just as present in the world as in the church we would have to admit to being less spiritual than we make ourselves out to be. Why? Because in the world we lose our spiritual sight. The mere fact that we set Christian things apart from the world is evidence of our inability and perhaps even our refusal to find God in everything. We even use this as a rationale for going to church— to get our focus back on the Lord—as if to assume that the world will take it off the Lord every time. And whose fault is that? If God can be found in the average activities of an average day, then we have no one but ourselves to blame for our inability to see him there.

I suspect that we like keeping these realms separate. Sometimes I wonder if it isn't as important for us to keep the world "secular" as it is to protect the sanctity of Christian things. What if the world isn't entirely "secular?" What if the world can be a holy place where God can be found? Well then, why aren't we finding him? Why aren't we even trying? Perhaps we like the excuse a worldly world offers us to drop our spiritual responsibilities and indulge in its seductions and devices. And I wonder if the preponderance of Christian goods and services hasn't added to this false perception and given us more reason to not seek God when indulging in worldly entertainment, work, or average everyday activities.

With so much Christian stuff available, it seems like anything that isn't "Christian" is devoid of God by default, which would include baseball, of course. Especially with all these high salaries and greedy people now dominating the sport. Certainly there couldn't be anything pure about baseball anymore.

Or could there be? It all depends on your insight. Michael O'Connor has found enough of it to write a book. Seems to me you could feel this way about a lot of things besides baseball. How many books are waiting to be written by Christians on the spiritual life of football, soccer, rock music, rock climbing, snowboarding, surfing, mathematics, politics, psychology, ballooning, driver training, gardening (it's been done)…and there would be no end to this list.

"I believe in two things." Michael says in his introduction, "God the Father, Son and Holy Spirit, Creator of Heaven and Earth, the beginning and the end, the Alpha and Omega, the one and only source from which all life flows—and baseball. Everything else is just sports and religion."

What do you love in life? Seems to me you could put just about anything in the place where Michael has baseball and find a connection and a way of reclaiming God's world for his glory and your enjoyment.

Everything else is just a category.

The Novelist Who Teaches Sunday School

In what was for him a rare public appearance, John Grisham (the prolific author of legal thrillers, six of which have been turned into blockbuster movies) spoke at a writing and poetry conference at Baylor University in Waco, Texas. As a Christian and a Sunday school teacher in his hometown Southern Baptist church, Grisham is on a short list of Christians whose works have gained a high level of exposure in popular culture. And Grisham hasn't exactly hidden his Christianity either. At least two of his stories have conversion experiences in them, and his 10th novel, *The Testament*, has a committed Christian missionary as a main character. With Baylor being a Southern Baptist institution, this lecture held the promise of hearing, for the first time in public, how, if at all, Grisham connects his faith and his work. He did not disappoint in his comments, though they may not have been what everyone was expecting.

Grisham was very emphatic during both his talk, and a question and answer period following, that he did not consider himself a Christian writer or a writer of Christian books. He was a story writer who happened to be a Christian. A Christian message, if there is going to be one, has to serve the story. He said that people who want to write suspense novels have to master that craft, with all of its ironic details and elaborate plot devices. Writers either learn how to do that, or they don't. Once someone has mastered the craft, then they can try to weave in a deeper message. It rarely works the other way around.

"The other way around" has been a *faux pas* for Christians ever since we started delving into contemporary art forms. Getting the message out has often been more important than getting the art right, which can result in a forced or manipulated version of the art in order to accommodate the message. Grisham is basically saying that if you want to have a novel that carries any kind of Christian message to the world, you better know first how to write a good novel. Master the art before you attempt the message.

To some, this might sound as though it makes the message secondary. It does not. It only gives the message a chance to be heard by those who need it most. Sacrifice the art, and you guarantee the message will be heard only by those who, because they already support it, are tolerant of any effort on its behalf. Those who don't care about the message have no such incentive.

The best blending of art and message should actually make you miss the message. That is, you are so caught up in the story, the film, or the song that you are not even aware the message is there. Not that it is absent or silent; it's just not waving a flag in your face. Sometimes the message is subtle and takes some effort to find. Sometimes the message is so big and true and real that you miss it for all its bigness, like staring at tree trunks and wondering where the forest is.

In the case of *The Testament*, the Christian character is an uncompromising missionary, Rachel Lane, who has sacrificed everything to carry the gospel to a tiny native tribe in the Amazon jungle. Sounds as boring as a missionary slide show. But what if this missionary suddenly inherited $11 billion? And what if some half-cocked, two-bit lawyer fresh from drug and alcohol rehab—and awash in the value systems that tempt all of us—had to go down to South America to find her and inform her of her fortune (and, of course, fall in love with her in the process)?

Suddenly this missionary thing makes for a darn good story.

Will she leave her tribe in the Amazon to enjoy her new-found wealth in the modern world? Would you? We live in a society that assumes there is a point when money obliterates all other values. Will she succumb to the love of someone who doesn't share her convictions? We live in a society that assumes there is a point where passion obliterates all other values. These are modern American beliefs. Many of us as Christians share them without knowing it. Is this a big enough message for a novelist with a Christian worldview? I think it's big enough for all of us.

Think of all the millions of people who have now read a story about a person who would rather see Christ manifested in the lives of a few people in a nameless Amazon jungle than submit to the passions of money and romance. This character not only confronts popularly held American values, she also confronts idolatries that tempt the best of us. Proof of how the truth can nail us before we ever even figure out whether something is Christian or not.

The House of Truth

My plane arrived in between two van loads shuttling conferees to downtown hotels, so I ordered a latte and a muffin and waited in the airport for the next group of artists to arrive. By the time I checked into my hotel, I only had time to retrieve my E-mail and phone messages and get to the opening night gala concert without picking up a registration packet. Late night showcases for new artists seemed to be advertised on every available wall space of the convention lobby, and handouts were already littering the floors.

But for artists and affiliates like Edward Wapp Wahpeconiah, Strawberry Moon Records and *Dirty Linen* magazine, this could easily be Gospel Music Association week in Nashville. Instead, it's a few hundred miles to the west, a few months earlier, and a lot more rugged in Albuquerque, New Mexico. This is the 11th annual Folk Alliance Conference, a national convention for the furtherance of folk music and dance.

It's a wide swath this eclectic grouping paints, from Peter Yarrow to specialists in American Indian music to Celtic bands and blues artists. Singer/songwriters proliferate, all looking for a chance to play their songs to any audience, even if it's a 1 a.m. showcase in a hotel room. They are here as much to network and share songs as they are to be discovered.

Folk music is a small market filled with brilliant young players who have made the discovery that there really does exist an audience for a singer/songwriter with a story to tell. Among these artists are some Christians who have been sharpening their craft in a grueling circuit of coffeehouses, bars, colleges, universities and house concerts—all small venues with enthusiastic audiences eager for an intimate experience of a venerable art form. A perusal of the convention material turns up names of such well-known believers in this trade as Bruce Cockburn, David Wilcox, Jan Krist, Pierce Pettis, Bob Franke and Brooks Williams as well as other newer names on the scene such as Christopher Williams, Skatman Meredith, Matt Auten and Steve Black. These Christians are creating music that defies categorization. This is music too good to be ignored, but not pop enough or lyrically Christian enough to have big commercial success in any market.

In the course of a few days I heard a song about Buddha and Mohammed on their way to a birthday party for Jesus, about a wrecking ball (of judgment) headed towards us all, about taking a journey to the house of truth, about how a woman in her forties is a force to be reckoned with, about a husband whose practical wife is "practically his," about a young mother rocking her baby in her grandmother's rocker that speaks a hundred memories to her, about how bright the light is, and about how, when contemplating an investigation of that light, you "…need not sign your life away just to take a look."

As a fellow artist, mentor, and representative of Christian music, I have to admit I was charmed by this music. I found music that, without naming God or Jesus or any identifiable Christian words and phrases, could reach to the spiritual heart of my being and elicit spontaneous praise. These artists are touching on spiritual truth without using overtly Christian lyrics, and I am convinced they are doing it not because they are ashamed of the gospel or to gain a bigger market, but because their own integrity and desire for fresh expression demands it.

This is music that will probably never meet the criteria of "Christian music," but will nonetheless be deeply rewarding to anyone willing to put forth an effort in finding it. Thanks to events like this, it may not be as hard as it once was.

Actually, I hope categorization becomes more and more difficult. One of these days we may be able to be done with definitions because we have learned to rejoice in truth wherever we find it. I have a hunch the house of truth, when we get there, will be bigger and have more rooms in it than we ever imagined.

Only a World to Reach

The event was a free birthday bash at the Starplex amphitheater in Dallas celebrating the anniversary of a local alternative rock station. The Dallas Morning News listed the groups to play that day as Cowboy Junkies, Jewel, Dada, Deep Blue Something, and Jars of Clay—"one of the few Christian groups that tons of non-Christians have actually heard."

The summer night air hung low and smoky from tobacco and some other leaves that were burning. I looked out over rows of shaved, cropped hairdos. The guy next to me had five earrings on his face and only two of them were actually on his ears. Two stagehands were lighting candelabras on either side of the large dark stage when a disk jockey from the local rock station came out and introduced the last group. "Ladies and gentlemen, a new group we happen to like a lot, and I know you will too. Please welcome… Jars of Clay!"

Under cover of fog and loud Gregorian chanting, six young men slipped on stage. Soon two acoustic guitarists emerged from the fog. The audience was on its feet—some standing on top of chairs, and some dancing in the aisles. Three layers of tight vocals mimicked the chanting and then the strains of the first lyric could be heard as the music backed off to let the words through: Arms nailed down, are you telling me something?

All I could think of was, "We've waited a long time for this." The guy next to me, the one with the facial jewelry, had been waiting all his life. "Are you with Jars?" he had asked when I first came in, probably noticing the backstage pass I had stuck on my chest.

"Yes," I said.

"If you're going to see them afterwards, would you thank them for me? I became a Christian listening to their CD."

"You mean, he got everything he needed to know to become a Christian off of one CD?" I asked myself.

"I played it over and over and figured out just about everything. I went and got a Christian friend of mine— pulled him out of a party—and told him I wanted to get saved right away. He didn't believe me. You wouldn't have either. I hated Christians."

Now here you have a guy who hated Christians, falling in love with music written and sung by Christians, and following the lyrics right up to the gospel. He went on to tell me he's now reading *Mere Christianity* by C.S. Lewis and wants to be a novelist.

Something about this seems fragile...breakable. Something tells me we need to back off and let this kind of thing happen. Unfortunately there were some Christians in the audience that night with the poor taste to cheer for Jesus. Someone please tell them this isn't a contest. There are no sides. There are only sinners and a gospel and people with lots of earrings who are finding ears for God they didn't know they had.

When contemporary Christian music started, it was a lot like this. You would have gone to hear a Christian group and smelled pot and sat next to someone who appeared at first to be as far from the kingdom of God as you could imagine, until you talked to him and found out he had just walked into it three weeks earlier. In 1970 there wasn't a Christian audience to entertain; there was only a world to reach. Now, at least a generation later, there still is.

CHAPTER SEVENTEEN

Declaration of a Fearless Christian

———— ❧ ————

You Are There, and You Are Not Hiding

Christians in America need an image overhaul. We need a new look. During the Jesus Movement in the early '70s we called ourselves "Jesus freaks" and "radicals for Christ." The gospel went out through organizations such as Christian World Liberation Front and Jesus People USA (still alive and well in Chicago). People got saved in such coffeehouses as The Salt Company and at festivals such as Sweet Jesus Roll Away the Stone (or Rock) Concert. New converts got their training at Jesus Christ Light and Power House.

Why all the crazy names? I think it was an attempt to say, "This isn't the Christianity you are used to. Whatever you thought Christians were like, think again. You better check out what's happening here because these people are something different." Of course a name doesn't mean much, but it shows that someone realized that a change in perception was needed. The old words did not communicate the reality of what Christ was really doing at the time.

I think it's time again—not for a name change, but an understanding change. Christ is doing a new work among us that doesn't fit the current impressions. In the '70s it was: Christians aren't boring, long-faced stick-in-the-muds with short hair and suits. Now it's: Christians aren't Bible-thumping conservatives with an agenda and an attitude. We need to let people know that we're not trying to take over the world; we're just here to help.

I hope we can change more than just an impression. It would be nice to change some lives. Wouldn't it be great if people who might not want to be around Christians might want to be around you? That can happen when they see something in you different from their usual impression of Christians.

They will see, first, that you are there and not hiding. They will see that you genuinely care about them and respect what they think and believe. They will see that when you talk about your faith and your relationship with Christ, you are merely opening your life to them, not reading them a script or following some prescribed course to get them converted. They will feel as if they are important in your life even if they do not agree with you.

A Personal Declaration

The following is a declaration I have drawn up for myself of what I mean when I call myself a Christian. It is not the final word on the subject, but a means of capsulizing some of the more important ways I want to think about the world and act in it. You may choose to adopt some or all of it as your own, and I hope you will add to it. I feel strongly about this. I would nail it to my door or wear it on my chest if I thought it would help, but I believe if I have it in my heart and act accordingly, that will be enough.

If we are going to be "in the world and not of it," as Christ has suggested, the current model of a Christian will not do. That model works only in a safe subculture. Outside, it is dangerous and undefined. Outside is the challenge. Outside are those waiting to be noticed and loved by Christians with a fearless enough faith to be there. I hope one of them is you.

Whereas: We are followers of Christ who are wary about things that are given the cultural label "Christian"; and

Whereas: "Christian" has become a term that has more to do with how one aligns oneself politically and socially, or how one behaves in relation to certain cultural mores, than it does with anything of the heart; and

Whereas: We want to be Christians—but with a new definition;

We have come to the following conclusions:

I am not trying to create a place of safety in the world. Instead, I have found a place in my heart where Christ dwells, and this gives me courage to face the world as it is.

I realize my overall purpose is not to change the world (that kind of thing is beyond my control), but it is to bring comfort, peace, warmth, love, and aid to people who are in the world, in the name of Jesus and his gospel.

Even if I were able to control the moral standards of society I understand that I would not further the cause of

Christ by making people better. In fact, I recognize a selfish motive in making a better world so I can have a safer environment in which to live and raise my own family. This gives no regard to the fact that "better" people without Christ still perish in their sins. A more moral society means little or nothing if people do not come into relationship with Christ.

I may not look or talk like a traditional Christian because I hang around non-Christians a lot and have learned to play down my differences rather than exploit them, as some Christians have before me. I have discovered that by identifying with sinners I am in a better position to introduce them to Christ than when I remain separate and aloof because I think I am "different" (which usually translates to "better" in their minds). The only people who are looking for perfect Christians to model their lives after are other Christians, those who have bought the lie that perfection is attainable.

I will not be offended by the language and behavior of non-Christians. I realize, because I know myself, that sinners sin. There is no reason to be appalled at this. If I were perfect and had no sin of my own, I could be appalled, but I am not without sin. The only thing that should offend me is the same thing that offended Jesus: self-righteous hypocrisy. I realize that in choosing to be offended by the normal behavior of non-Christians, I am turning myself into the very thing Jesus hated. I, who am worried about being offended, make myself an offense to God.

I have decided not to put any real stock in having famous people endorse Jesus and have concluded I would be happier having Jesus endorse me. Character is superior to fame and glory.

I realize that I live in a world dominated by secular minds and philosophies. Because of my love for all people and my desire for them to know the love of Christ, I choose to learn about and interact with these philosophies rather than categorically reject them. When it becomes obvious that I do have to part ways with the world to avoid compromise of our beliefs, I will do this in such a way as to not judge others who don't feel as I do.

Though my heart is connected to eternity, my feet are firmly planted on the earth. For this reason I will strategize, barter, study, and grow in two kingdoms. I have found that these two kingdoms need not always be warring against each other. I have found the things of God in the earthly world, and I have found evil in the kingdom of heaven, just as the parables of Jesus indicated I would.[1]

I have learned to appreciate the artistic expressions of those who are not following Christ. I will not begin with the assumption that they are wrong so that I can condemn them, but with the belief that they are right about something so that I can communicate with those who value their work.

I will not be threatened by "other paths to God" knowing that there is only one God and one way, and if people are truly seeking him, they will ultimately find their way to Christ even if they started out by way of another path.

I believe that wherever I go, God got there first. This means at least three things:

1. There is always something to find and embrace out in the world, since God's truth is everywhere.

2. There is nothing to fear because there is nowhere I can go on earth or in the heavens where God is not present.

3. There are many shoulders people are riding on other than my own. I do not have to finish everyone's

search; I am merely helping them along the way. If I happen to be there when someone comes to Christ, I will be overjoyed, but I will realize I am just one in a long line of witnesses who have prepared the way.

It is for these and other reasons that I do not need a host of Christian products to identify myself as a Christian. I want my life and my faith to speak for itself.

I do not have to determine whether a person is a Christian or a non-Christian before I know how to talk with him or her. Some may be drawn to me; others may be repelled. I do not know who is who—nor is it my responsibility to figure this out; I only point the way.

I can be fearless in the world because I know that Jesus is praying for my protection, and there is no one and no power on earth or in heaven that can stand against his will.

Therefore, and for all these reasons, I do not have to hide in a Christian subculture, nor do I have to spend all my efforts to fight society. I am not at war with the world. I love the world as God does because it is full of people for whom he gave his Son so that those who believe in him might not perish but have everlasting life.

Since Jesus did not come into the world to condemn it, neither will I. And since, instead, Jesus came to save the world, I will put all my efforts to that end, knowing that he has already completed all the work necessary to save people. What is left for me is to let them know.

When fear rules, it's because deep down I don't believe I have what it takes to face the danger. The excitement comes in knowing and believing that through his Holy Spirit in me, I do.

SIGNED: _____

Notes

Chapter One—The Prayer of Jesus

1. Todd Hahn and David Verhaagen, *Gen Xers After God* (Grand Rapids: Baker, 1998), p. 62.

Chapter Two—Spiritual Microclimate

1. Jim Taylor and Watts Wacker, *The 500-Year Delta* (San Francisco: Harperbusiness, 1997).
2. Thomas C. Reeves, "Not So Christian America," *First Things*, October 1996.
3. Natalie Angier, "Confessions of a Lonely Atheist," *Los Angeles Times*, January 2001.
4. Ibid.

Chapter Three—What Are We Really Saying?

1. William Lobdell, "Mariners Plans to Put the 'Mega' Into 'Mega Church,'" *Los Angeles Times,* May 17, 2001, p. B12.

Chapter Five—Wading into Shallow Water

1. Mark Heard, "Orphans of God," from the album, *Satellite Sky* (Fingerprint Records, 1992). Used by permission.
2. Mark Heard, "Stuck in the Middle," from the album, *Stop the Dominoes,* (Home Sweet Home Records, 1981). Used by permission.
3. Sheldon Vanauken, *A Severe Mercy* (Harper & Row: San Francisco, 1977), p. 77.
4. "Fans Say Good-bye," *CCM Magazine,* November 1997, p. 56.

Chapter Seven—Against the World

1. Hanna Rosin, "God's Hit Man," *GQ*, January 1999, p. 114.
2. Stephen L. Carter, *God's Name in Vain* (New York: Basic Books, 2000).
3. Hanna Rosin, ibid., p. 146.

Chapter Eight—The Fundamental Element of Safety

1. Mike Boehm, "Twist of Faith: Christian Punk Bands Struggle to Define Their Evangelical Roles," *Los Angeles Times,* June 10, 1998, p. F2.

Chapter Nine—It's a Jungle Out There

1. Keith Willhite, Scott M. Gibson, Haddon W. Robinson, eds., *The Big Idea of Biblical Preaching* (Grand Rapids: Baker, 1999), p. 84.
2. Marc Gunther, "God and Business," *Fortune*, July 9, 2001, p. 59.

Chapter Ten—Coming Out

1. Gavin Bryars, "Jesus' Blood Never Failed Me Yet," Point Music, a division of Poly-Gram Records, 1993, from the liner notes.
2. Ibid.
3. It seems to have escaped the notice of many Christians that Johnny Cash has published a book titled *Man in White*, a novel dealing with the conversion of Saul to Paul the apostle. The book was researched and written by Cash himself and reveals a very deep knowledge of Scripture, salvation, and the early days of the Christian faith.
4. Jancee Dunn, "Johnny Cash," *Rolling Stone,* June 30, 1994, p. 35.

Chapter Eleven—Gaining Credibility

1. Mary Cagney, "Why Hollywood Doesn't Like You," *Christianity Today,* August 10, 1998, p. 64.
2. Ibid.
3. C.S. Lewis, *God in the Dock* (Grand Rapids, Michigan: Eerdmans, 1970), p. 93.

Chapter Twelve—If There Were No Christian World

1. Mark Joseph, *Rock and Roll Rebellion* (Nashville: Broadmann and Holman, 1999).
2. Gunther "God and Business," Ibid.

Chapter Fourteen—"It's Over. Go Home."

1. Oswald Chambers, *My Utmost for His Highest* (New York: Dodd Mead and Co., 1935), p. 350.
2. 2 Corinthians 5:1-10 is a great discussion of the implications of the temporary nature of our faith.

Chapter Fifteen—Evangelism 101

1. From "The Only Way," by John Fischer on his Silent Planet recording "Some Folks World." Silent Planet Records, Raleigh, North Carolina, www.silentplanetrecords.com.

Chapter Sixteen—Snapshots: Fearless Faith in Action

1. Michael O'Conner, *Sermon on the Mound* (Minneapolis: Bethany House, 2001), p. 19.

Chapter Seventeen—Declaration of a Fearless Christian

1.   Three of the parables found in Matthew 13 deal with evil in the kingdom of heaven. They all begin with, "The kingdom of heaven is like…" The first is the most obvious (verses 24 to 30), about the man who sowed good seed in his field and then his enemy came and sowed weeds while he was sleeping. The second is about a mustard seed that grows into a large tree (verses 31 to 32). Some scholars interpret this as being abnormal growth. And then there is the parable of the yeast that was mixed into a large amount of flour and worked its way through the whole of the dough (verse 34). Yeast was always a symbol of sin. The Jews are to eat unleavened bread. "Beware the leaven of the Pharisees." The only reasonable conclusion to these stories is that he is speaking to the kingdom of heaven on earth, or what is now called the church. Few would question the presence of evil in the church. Still, that does not make it any less God's agent in the world for bringing his truth.

About the Author

———— ✒ ————

John Fischer is one of contemporary Christian music's founding fathers. His best-known songs from the '60s and '70s are "The All Day Song" (or "Love Him in the Morning"), "Have You Seen Jesus My Lord?" and "Look All Around You."

Along with his 12 albums, John has authored 12 books, including the bestseller *Real Christians Don't Dance* and the popular fiction novel *Saint Ben.*

John now lectures at Christian colleges, speaks and sings at retreats and churches, and writes several columns: a monthly one for Charles Colson's Breakpoint.org, a bimonthly one for the new Walk Thru the Bible devotional *InDeed,* and the award-winning "Consider This…" for *CCM Magazine.* His articles have appeared in numerous Christian periodicals, including *Moody Monthly, Discipleship Journal,* and *Decision* magazines.

John lives in Laguna Beach, California, with his wife, Marti, and their newly adopted two-year-old, Chandler. Two older children, Christopher and Anne, are in college and postgraduate studies.

For more information on John, visit his Web site at www.fischtank.com